CW00542720

RAB WILSON is one of Scotland's most
born in New Cumnock, Ayrshire in
apprenticeship with the National (
following the Miners' Strike of 1984
nurse, spending the next 27 years in t
becoming a front page whistleblower in the NHS after exposing a
national scandal at NHS Ayrshire & Arran. He was widely lauded
and praised in the press, TV and radio for his bravery in this action.
He is still very much involved as an activist for social justice.

As a Scots poet, his work has appeared regularly in *The Herald*,
Chapman, *Lallans* and *Southlight* magazines and he is the author
of a number of highly praised volumes of poetry and a Burns
scholar. Rab has performed his work at the Edinburgh Festival,
the StAnza poetry festival at St Andrews, the Burns an a' That
Festival at Ayr and has been 'Bard of the Festival' at Wigtown,
Scotland's National Booktown. Rab is a previous winner of the
McCash Poetry Prize and was 'Robert Burns Writing Fellow –
In Reading Scots' for Dumfries and Galloway Region. He has
worked with the artist Calum Colvin on a book of responses to
Burns and has been Scriever-in-Residence for the National Trust
for Scotland based at the Robert Burns Birthplace Museum in
Alloway. Rab is currently Preses for the Scots Leid Associe/Scots
Language Association. In 2023 he was one of the recipients of
the Andrew Fletcher of Saltoun Award, Scotland's highest public
award for Arts & Humanities. He is a 'weel-kent' advocate for
Scots language and writing. He lives in New Cumnock with his
wife Margaret.

By the same author:

The Ruba'iyat of Omar Khayyam in Scots, Luath Press, 2004
Accent o the Mind, Luath Press, 2006
Life Sentence, Luath Press, 2008
A Map for the Blind, Luath Press, 20011
Oor Big Braw Cosmos (with the late John C Brown, Astronomer Royal for Scotland), Luath Press, 2019
Burnsiana (with Calum Colvin), Luath Press, 2020
Zero Hours, Luath Press, 2020

Collier Laddie

RAB WILSON

Luath Press Limited

EDINBURGH

www.luath.co.uk

First published 2024

ISBN: 978-1-80425-134-8

The author's right to be identified as author of this book
under the Copyright, Designs and Patents Act 1988 has been asserted.

The paper used in this book is recyclable. It is made from
low-chlorine pulps produced in a low-energy, low-emission
manner from renewable forests.

Printed and bound by
Robertson Printers, Forfar

Typeset in 10.5 point Sabon LT by
Main Point Books, Edinburgh

*This book is fondly dedicated to all the comrades
I worked with at Barony Colliery, Auchinleck.*

Contents

PART 2: COME ALL YE BOLD MINERS

CONTENTS

Introduction

TUCKED AWAY IN the loft of my house there is an old battered blue suitcase. I seldom look at this suitcase or pay any attention to it. It contains another life from long ago. Very occasionally, if I happen to be in the loft I might have a quick peek inside it, then close it again. It contains some old T-shirts, a pair of worn-out Levi jeans, patched and faded, with cloth sew-on badges with names of rock bands on them... from when I was a teenage Punk rocker. There's a wooden cigar box, filled with stubs of concert tickets; The Clash; Siouxsie and the Banshees; Magazine; the Buzzcocks; David Bowie... and button badges bearing the names of such groups. But mostly, the case is filled with lots of old newspapers... bags of letters... curious ephemera and paperwork... and three A5 desk diaries that measure 5.8 x 8.3 inches... I was a child of the imperial system... the newspapers and letters pertain to an event that I took part in 40 years ago...

This book contains edited extracts from these diaries that I kept...

I want to tell you a story... but first of all, I need to set the scene...

When I was a young man, at the fag-end of the 1970s, I began an engineering apprenticeship in the Scottish coal mining industry, at Barony Colliery, East Ayrshire. The indentured apprenticeship agreement, on its formal legalese document, with National Coal Board green heraldic crest stamped at the top, states the date of commencement as 8 August 1977. I wasn't really cut-out to be an engineer, but having no real plan in life, like many young men at the time, getting a 'good trade' was something parents greatly encouraged. I think I managed to fail most of the important exams the coal board and technical college devised for me… and in 1981, after five miserable attempts, also failed in my final exams. I was then allocated to menial work as a fitter's mate, helping to maintain the heavy engineering equipment that allowed mine cars full of coal to be rammed off the winding cages, shunted round a short 'railway' type gravity system, emptied of their precious cargo onto gigantic conveyor belts, then in their circuitous route be returned back onto the winding cages, returned down the pit to be filled again and again in their interminable filling and emptying journey, supplying the country with vital coal and energy. It could at times be gruelling and dirty work maintaining this often dangerous machinery.

The upside of the job was the camaraderie, people you worked with, lifelong friendships made, and the sense of fun, carry-on, practical jokes and unique sense of humour that permeated the coal mining industry; humour as black as the seams of coal that were daily hewed. The 'closeness' of the human bond, formed over centuries, in mining communities.

This was my working life for almost ten years. I of course had a life outside the pit. I was the middle of three kids; my older brother Jim had already qualified as a mining engineer – he was, and still is, the model of a journeyman tradesman, highly skilled and technically gifted – my younger sister Laura trained as a nurse with the NHS, and now decades later, is a qualified Cognitive Behavioural Therapist – but I was the 'difficult' middle child! My family lived on a 10-acre smallholding, Polquhirter Nursery in New Cumnock, that my grandfather sweated to buy in the 1930s. Mum was an only child. She was brought up to take over and run the nursery – sent to London in the Coronation year of 1952 to train as a florist at the school ran by the great Constance Spry – she married my dad, a local musician, and they grew the business. They built 17 huge industrial greenhouses, filled with tomato plants, then later, flowers, and had a fruit &

veg business... we had a lorry and one of the last horse & cart businesses in Ayrshire. Dad died when I was 21. Mum married my stepfather – whom I did not get on with. I helped out with the family business (as did my brother & sister) delivering flowers and arrangements for weddings & occasions, and wreaths for local funerals. We would take orders on the phone on Interflora from all round the world. The family were all quite musical... I was musical... my father resurrected the local silver band and I played solo cornet in it. I also played keyboards. I had great visions of being a pop star – like many delusional young people! Though I did play in many successful local 'covers bands', performing in the many pubs, hotels, working men's clubs and miners clubs that existed all over the area. The family business thrived, local factories boomed, the pits brought in good wages and were the mainstay of all local industry and commerce... village life in Ayrshire revolved round the vast mining industry. Life was pretty good for working people.

Then, in 1984, we had the great Miners' Strike.

Just like the Martians in HG Wells' *War of the Worlds*, plotting in secret to destroy the Earth, we also had deadly enemies plotting in secret in Downing Street to destroy the mining industry. And destroy it they did...

A long time after these events I became a well-published poet. Also, a long time after these events, I began to write poems that recorded and reflected on my time in the mining industry; some relating to the history of the industry; humorous 'Tam o'Shanter-esque' narrative verse, recording events at work; the Miners' Strike itself; and pre- and post-Strike mining/industrial related poetry. This book contains many of these writings and – 40 years after the events – my personal account of a national event that rocked the UK's industrial fabric to its foundations. It's a local reflection on national events. Thousands upon thousands of people will have their own memories, experiences and views of the Miners' Strike and the mining way of life, but this book contains mine, as expressed through the prism of my poetry and diaries.

I have edited the diary extracts; there were many references in them to personal relationships, mundane family events and daily life, that I have mostly left out… it is mainly a record of how the Strike progressed, and its effects nationally and locally where I lived. Many, many people's lives were changed irrevocably and forever due to the Strike. People died. People were killed.

The industry I spent the first ten years of my working life in was completely erased from the landscape. It exists now in books like this, or in museums. Odd physical traces of it remain; the huge Barony 'A' Frame winding headgear at Auchinleck, bestriding the earth like Ted Hughes giant 'Iron Man'; the Newtongrange Mining Museum; the scars on hillsides and man-made lochans from abandoned opencast sites… fading into history… I left the mining industry on Friday 31 January 1986, and commenced training as a psychiatric staff nurse at the Crichton Royal Hospital, Dumfries, on Monday 3 February 1986. I could not afford to take a holiday or break between ending one career and starting another.

At the end of my shift on that last Friday in January I took off my worn, steel-capped pit boots, my old 1950s style corrugated miner's helmet, carried them to the 'dirt-hopper' conveyor belt, dropped them onto it, and watched them slowly disappear into darkness… I then walked to the baths in my stocking soles, showered, boarded the pit bus, went home, and never went back to the pit again.

Rab Wilson
February 2024

Note

PART 1 CONSISTS of extracts from a daily diary kept by the author throughout the Miners' Strike 1984–85. It also includes sonnets inspired by individuals who took part in the Strike, featured in Joe Owens's book, *Miners 1984–1994: A Decade of Endurance*.

Parts 2 and 4 consist of poems written over many years – social and political musings relating to mining in Scotland.

Part 3 consists of humorous rhyming poems written in a style typical of poetry that used to be penned by many ordinary pit workers and rhymers. These poems were inspired by the Barony Colliery, Auchinleck, the people who worked there and events that took place.

Part 5 is a section of new poems examining the legacy of the Miners' Strike and the effect it still has on former Scottish mining communities 40 years after the event.

Prologue

Here We Go, Here We Go, Here We Go...

Victorious warriors win first and then go to war, while defeated warriors go to war first and then seek to win—Sun Tzu, *The Art of War*

Ootside the baths we shuffled oor feet,
freezin fog happit ower the Horrals,
the pitheid lik an L.S. Lowry pentin,
else, some auld black an white Victorian photie.
Mairch; snell, cranreuch, bitin cauld,
haunds thrust deeply intae poackets,
bunnets pu'd doun ower oor lugs,
we waitit.
Forty or fifty men, piece bags slung,
towels rowed up, unner wir oxters,
braith expelled in cloods;
stirks in a slauchterhoose pen.
Then, the union guy appeared,
an stuid oan the wa, forenenst the canteen.
He tellt us fair an square the die wis cast,
the Yorkshire boys aareadies aa wir oot,
an syne the feck o us wid dae the same.
Some muttert aiths ablow their braith,
ithers stared at naethin.
The aulder heids amang thaim bowcht a bit,
they'd bin here afore; kent whit wis comin.
Across the caur-park twa-three craws
wir pickin at an empty paper pock.
Some young yins lauched an joked –
their een wid suin be opened.
Ah spake oot, an said it wid be folly,
but naebody peyed me ony mind.
An thon's hou it stairts,
thon's hou it ayeweys stairts.

PART ONE

The Enemy Within...?

Monday 30 January 1984
Monday morning again. Bobby England's on dayshift with us this week. He has got his date to retire, in March I think? Soon there'll be none of the old team left; old Harry Parker died last October; Hughie Ritchie retired last summer, and now Bobby...! The backshift's tokens were all lifted at the Time Hall and all the miners went back home in sympathy with the men from E21 Face. I don't know how this will affect us tomorrow on the day shift. This evening I watched a documentary about Scott Lithgow's shipyard closing down, it reminded me of the pits... (4,000 men went home today, half the Scottish workforce, because of the Overtime Ban). This Government is bringing Scotland to its knees. In a few years I don't think there'll be much left up here.

Tuesday 31 January 1984
Arrived at work to find large crowd of workers assembled outside the pit baths. There must have been over a hundred men. The dispute had carried on from yesterday, and most of the miners (Group 1) all went back home. Myself, still being in the Tradesmen's Union (Group 2) was able to attend my work. Out of about 400 men about 50 were working. Little Hughie Allan took a lot of stick because he worked (he is a Group 1 man). The 24-Hour Warning was put into effect, so I don't know whether we will be working tomorrow or not.

Wednesday 8 February 1984
Surprisingly, we were all working at the colliery today. The coal cutting machine that had broken down was brought up to the surface, and anyone who was anyone was gathered round it to try and find out what had gone wrong with it. I'm not sure yet as to what was exactly wrong with it! Otherwise, quite a quiet day for me again. There was a pit-head meeting at 2:30pm. The Area Union Executive were there, and Neilly Valentine, the Group 2

delegate from Lugar, was there as well. They told the assembled crowd of miners (about 100 in all) that the Government was out to destroy the mining industry in Scotland, and that the pits that had been closed down were not really exhausted and that they had plentiful working reserves of coal left. Neilly Valentine then gave a rousing patriotic speech about this being a fight to save Scotland's pits for our children, and so on… He warned us that we could be the next to go, along with Polmaise, Cardowan and Bogside ollieries… Scott Lithgow, Ravenscraig, Bathgate and numerous other firms who had went to the wall.

Monday 13 February, 1984
Routine day at work. Men from Killoch were picketing at Barony today. The men at Seafield Colliery have went on Strike calling for an all-out stoppage in Scotland. I'll have to wait till tomorrow to find out what course of action we'll be taking.

Alex Shanks, Edinburgh

Ah wis oan Newcraighall Strike Committee
A single mither wi next tae zero
Gied us a fiver oot o her giro
Men gied us free beer fae Dryborough Brewery.
The right tae work, that wis aa that we asked
Demands which the Tories said went too faur
Fir tellys, holidays, mibbes a caur
Sae judges an lawyers taen us tae task.
Ah wis dragged through the courts, heavily fined
An haen nae previous wis nae defence
Fined twa hunner pound fir a first offence
Aa ah did wis staun oan a picket line.
Ah'll nevvir forget it, it's left its mark,
It festers there yet, somewhaur in the daurk.

Billy Hodge, Cumnock

Gaun doon the Pits wis an easy road oot
Ma faimily aa went sae ah went tae
Ah wis deeply involved wi the Strike, nae
Qualms, fir a year it wis ma main pursuit.
We went wir ain road an ah'm proud tae say
The hale community pued thegither
A band o comrades, cared fir each ither
We raised oor ain funds an peyed oor ain way.
Pits huv been the wey o life aroond here
Fowk wha owned pubs earnt money fae miners
Fowk wha hud shops earnt money fae miners
Noo we kin haurdly afford tae buy beer.
We'll nevvir win back whit the Tories took
The future? This isnae the place tae look.

Monday 5 March, 1984
Lot of work piled up today. The mine car tippler main bearings collapsed, that caused a lot of problems. Went down pit with John Gibson to work on inset level creepers. It was terrible. I had to lie in mud about 8 inches deep and my boots were full of stinking water. Afterwards I felt really disgusted about the conditions we have to work in sometimes. We scraped the muck, which was clinging in lumps to my boiler suit, off with old hacksaw blades, then I had to mix sand with Swarfega to get the dirt off my hands. On the news, Yorkshire Coalfield has called a Strike starting from next weekend. I'll probably hear tomorrow how this will affect us.

Tuesday 6 March, 1984
Busy again today. Nearly slept in. Windows at Time Office (where we lift our tokens) were closed at ten to seven. John Stirling, the personnel manager, didn't look too pleased. Creeper chain broke on Bottom Level, spent about three and a half hours down pit repairing it. Heavy, gruelling, dirty work. It would've been worse but they weren't winding coal though because they were replacing the main bearings on the coal tippler up on the pit-head. Fell out with Alex McLatchie the banksman again. I find it really difficult to get on with that guy. Came home knackered at 3pm. Heard that they have called for a National Strike in Scotland from Friday. God knows what'll happen now. I hope we get working a full week this week or my finances could hit trouble.

Wednesday 7 March, 1984
Got up a bit earlier today. Another gruelling shift fitting chain to inset level chain creeper. I was covered in greasy muck from head to foot. We worked at it for nearly the whole shift. We got it on eventually though. I finished early, at 1:30pm. It took me ages to get cleaned up. Came home

and went to bed for a couple of hours.

Thursday 8 March, 1984
Finished creeper job today then spent a slightly easier day
on pit-head. No more word yet on whether we are Striking.
There's to be a pit-head meeting tomorrow. I lifted £10 from
the bank, but I'll need to watch my finances for a while.

Friday 9 March, 1984
Had to go down pit today to change piston assembly on
inset-dip off-going cylinder. Was cold and wet. Rest of shift
wasn't so bad though. Alex Peters (deputy chief engineer)
came in and gave me a row for sitting about at 1:30pm.
The men had a show of hands today and voted to work on
Monday. I'm undecided though, but I won't cross a picket
line if it comes to the crunch.

Jim Armitage, Fallin

Ah worked as a coalcutting machineman
Ah worked wi ma faither fir fourteen year
But eftir the Strike it suin became clear
There'd be nae mercy fae Wheelers henchmen.
Fifty year auld, an ye're oan the scrapheap
Ah've mind ah walked owre that bing every day
It taen juist three months tae clear it away
Ninety years o toil, gone fae the landscape.
An ah've mind this section, that man, this run
The camaraderie, the boys ah knew
A wheen o them's away, deid and gone noo
Ah've mind o the laughs we hud, an the fun.
Ah tried tae write a book, aboot the Pit,
Ah managed twa pages, an that wis it.

Sunday 11 March, 1984
Arthur Scargill was on *Weekend World* today. He put up a good case for Strike action. I won't be working tomorrow. Went to cinema at Ayr tonight, an American comedy titled *Risky Business* was on. It was very good.

Monday 12 March, 1984
My first day on Strike. Got up about 10am. Did some flower order deliveries for Mum. Passed Barony Colliery gates about 2pm. There were quite a few pickets, some police and a TV camera. The dayshift had virtually all worked, but the backshift went home. I don't think anyone will be working tomorrow.

Tuesday 13 March, 1984
Strike seems to be taking more effect now. I don't think any pits in Scotland were working today. The television showed scenes from pit gates in Nottingham, Wales and Scotland. There's some mixed feelings among the men, especially in Nottingham, but they make big wages there so they'll be the last to come out probably, they're having a secret ballot there on Friday.

Wednesday 14 March, 1984
The *News at One* said that the NCB (National Coal Board) had applied for a High Court injunction to prevent NUM (National Union of Mineworkers) pickets from Yorkshire picketing pits in Nottingham. There was a lot of violent picketing at pits in England and at Bilston Glen in Scotland.

Thursday 15 March, 1984
A miner was killed on a picket line in Yorkshire, the cause seems a bit of a mystery though. The NUM says they will carry on with illegal flying pickets.

Wednesday 21 March, 1984

Went up the town to see what was happening. The Working Men's Club was closed. Seemingly it's closed Tuesday and Wednesday mornings. Stood at Tally's Café for a while with 'Cocky' Whiteford and Big John McKnight. There were a lot of miners gathered at the shelter next to the Pigeon Club, they were waiting for claim forms to help them pay their rent. A car-load of pickets arrived, they were getting a free meal at the Pigeon Club. Nationwide, the Strike is carrying on. There was a family from Yorkshire on telly, they were finding things hard and had to start rationing their food. The police are still trying to stop pickets from leaving one area to picket another.

Margaret Armitage, Fallin

The Fallin weemin formed a committee,
We caa'd wirsels Polmaise Wives Support Group,
We ran wee prize bingos, provided soup,
An chairged fowk sae much, it made funds ye see
Weemin were empowered an that wis new
Ah stood oan platforms, gied speeches an talks
Christ, ah even appeared twice oan the box
Ah'd confidence tae air ma point o view
We stood shooder tae shooder wi the men.
Ah've kept aa ma books an things fae the Strike
Ah'll nevvir pairt wi them, naw nevvir like,
Ah wid dae the same things aa owre again.
The wheel o village life spun roond the Pit,
When they taen away the hub, that wis it.

Tuesday 27 March, 1984

The Miners' Strike is still going on. This will be my third week without working. Some pits in Nottingham and Derby still working, but power stations are getting low on stocks now because the NUR (National Union of Railwaymen) and ASLEF (the train drivers' union) won't transport supplies of coal in. Domestic coal is in short supply now as well, people are running around gathering wood and coal wherever they can get it.

Wednesday 28 March, 1984

Heard on radio that Mick McGahey (Scottish Secretary NUM) was to appear at Cumnock Town Hall tonight. I went to the meeting. There were miners there from all over, the majority being from Killoch and Barony Collieries. There were about 500 people there – the hall was packed. George Foulkes MP, Mick McGahey, Neilly Valentine from Lugar Workshop and David Shankland, Labour Councillor from Cumnock and Doon Valley were at the main table on the stage. There was good order at the meeting and George Foulkes gave a rousing speech declaring the Labour party's support for the miners. Mick McGahey came on and told everyone about the NCB's plan to close pits, and said that this Strike was a struggle for the whole of Scotland. He put the case for the Strike and even asked for a show of hands for a Ballot, only a dozen or so raised their hands. When he then asked how many would picket Nottingham nearly everyone raised their hands. McGahey got a deserved standing ovation when he sat down.

Monday 2 April, 1984

Got up 9am. Got dressed and went out into garden to Creosote the fence. That took a couple of hours. Afterwards I went cycling. I went up through Burnfoot, past Dalleagles and took backroad past Dalgig to Benston Smiddy. It was a beautiful day, haven't felt so good for a while. Saw a lamb that had just been born, watched as it took its first steps. Came back in the Boig Road, there was only one picket on duty at Knockshinnoch coal washing plant, but it's not really in production yet anyway. There were quite a few people out on the old coal Bings with bags, digging for pieces of coal.

Tuesday 24 April, 1984
Got up 10am. Another glorious day. Went out on my pushbike. Went up to head of Afton Valley first – the sun was brilliant. On way back met Sandy McLatchie, who used to work at Barony Colliery. We watched the crowd of people who were digging for coal on the Bing, there must've been about 30 of them, they've flung up big mounds of dirt all over the place. A store of coal had got stolen from behind the Coach House Hotel in New Cumnock. The Coal Board seem to have made the first move today by saying that they would postpone pit closures, but the Union aren't too happy yet.

Dave Maguire, Auchinleck

They stairted back oan the Tuesday moarnin
Ah stairted back the followin Tuesday
Then they shut the Pit doon, it's aa away
Scargill wis richt, he gied us a warnin
Said in ten years there'd be nuthin left here
Ablow the brig there's no even a shop
Cept fir the Chinky, an neds smoking dope
It's no the same, no the same atmosphere
Mibbes ah'm depressed but whit dae ye dae
There's nuthin tae dae, nae use complainin
Whaur ur ye gonnae go when it's rainin
Ah'm feenished wi work, ah'm by wi life tae.
When the Pits were gaun this place wis alive
Scargill gied us ten, its only been five.

Friday 27 April, 1984

Arthur Scargill had been on the picket line in Nottingham with the Yorkshire miners. He has called for a Trade Union Rally in Nottingham, and is asking for all the mining pickets to descend on the Notts pits that are still working. The young single men are all feeling the pinch. They were handing out £10 each from the DHSS (Department of Health and Social Security) for them today at the community centre. There was a big queue of them waiting for money. I think the Labour party is beginning to get cold feet about supporting the miners, although they have called for all trade union members to donate 50p a week into a Strike Hardship Fund. I honestly don't know what will happen now at all, it's rumoured that our redundancy notices are waiting at Lugar Coal Board offices.

8th Week of Strike

Thursday 3 May, 1984

On the news, Ian MacGregor (the NCB Chairman) says he has no plans to change his policy, and there were big clashes between police and pickets at Nottingham, and at the steelworks at Ravenscraig and the power station at Hunterston. The general feeling is one of dejection among the miners, we don't seem to be anywhere nearer a settlement. The NCB also seem to have opened a phone-in for redundancies, a sneaky move, but no doubt among the older members of the workforce there'll be some amount of takers.

Thursday 10 May, 1984

The Strike drags on... about 60 miners were arrested at Hunterston power station in North Ayrshire today. They were trying to prevent the coal lorries from getting in. It was also the TUC (Scottish Trades Union Congress) 'Day of Action' and most of the buses, rail services, factories and other industries carried out a one day stoppage in support of the miners. The usual questions were asked on Robin Day's *Question Time*, but we still don't seem to be making any progress. Our leaders say we are winning though, so maybe it's just the media who are conning us? I just don't know who to believe. I need to keep a careful eye on my finances.

Wednesday 16 May, 1984
Arthur Scargill's wife was arrested on picket duty, they say the Strike could last to November. Mum says that 400 holidays have been cancelled at AT Mays, the local travel agents in Cumnock. The media do seem to be getting pretty hysterical though, and maybe if we just hold out then the miners will win the Strike, some folk must be feeling it pretty hard by now though.

Tuesday 29 May, 1984
In the news, there was a big picket at a coking plant near Scunthorpe today. About 50 miners were arrested. Police were flown in from about six counties, there were mounted police and men with riot shields and some pretty ugly, violent scenes. Talks are supposed to resume tomorrow to try and end the dispute. So far they haven't met with any success though.

Alex McCallum, Fallin

Ah goat sacked at the sit-in doon Polmaise
Sacked, fir juist waantin the pit tae survive
The gaffers haun't me ma P45
But ah've hud tae battle hard aa ma days.
When ah think o they men flung oan the Dole
Auld Bobby wis sixty, he'd taen a stroke
We focht his case, ah hope they bastarts choke
They refused tae even gie him his coal
But that's hou bad it wis. Eftir the Strike
Ah struggled fir work, blacklisted until
We baith goat joabs wi the local Cooncil.
The wife stood by me, ask her whit it's like
Nae joab security, leevin in fear
An we'd hoped tae hae a wee brek this year.

12th Week of Strike

Wednesday 30 May, 1984

The name of the coking plant is Orgreave. Arthur Scargill was arrested today outside the coking plant. The media, news, TV and papers were calling blue murder about the miners on the telly. There were really violent scenes, with horses charging into the miners. How a supposedly civilised country can allow such things to happen is beyond me, it makes me wonder if we have really progressed at all in the past two thousand years. Received letter from Barony Colliery today expressing serious state of deteriorating workings at pit.

Thursday 31 May, 1984

Called in at Cumnock Job Centre. They are getting nursing application forms in tomorrow for the 1985 intake, so I think I'll apply for that. Coal Board and NUM met for two and a half hours today. Ian MacGregor wasn't present. The talks are continuing painfully slowly.

Friday 1 June, 1984

Went to Cumnock Job Centre, 11am, and got application form for nursing. I don't know whether I'll be really suited for nursing, but job options are really limited. The intake isn't till next year anyway, so I'll have plenty of time to decide. Also, I wrote away for a salespersons job at Gauld's car showroom at Stewarton. I don't like these big upheavals in work but due to the Strike it is time I gave careful consideration as to my future. The clashes at Orgreave coking plant continued today. Police and pickets were back putting the boot in, it was disgusting to watch on telly. (Money getting low, had to count money bottle which I had intended to keep for holidays. There was £108 in it. I'll have to bank it on Monday.)

Tuesday 5 June, 1984

Watched programme *People to People*, which I'd taped night before off Channel 4. It was about how a local community in Yorkshire were facing up to the Strike. It showed you them being turned back by the police, who would give no reasons for their actions, and another guy asking a policeman if he could cross the road to remove his car. The policemen ignored him, and wouldn't answer him either. It really made my blood boil to see how the media were manipulating the situation to suit themselves. Heard on car radio that Barony Colliery was facing imminent threat of closure, it felt as though a great ship had just been sunk. It was a terrible feeling, although it seemed this had always been on the cards.

Wednesday 6 June, 1984

Went to Strike Centre for a while. Some of the lads were arranging to go to London to lobby Parliament on Thursday.

Martha McCallum, Fallin

Ah hale-heartedly agreed wi the Strike
It broke ma heart when they shut doon the Pit
Ah mean ah juist gret an gret aboot it
The miners' principles, ah thocht, wir right.
The Strike ruined us here, ah'll tell ye whit
Ah taen wee joabs cleanin an that, ye know
Tae pey the telly an the video
A hard road, an nae twae weys aboot it.
Ah hate the Polis noo, ken whit ah'm sayin
True, miners didnae act wi perfect grace
But whit they did wis a total disgrace
Ah'll nevvir be the same wi them again.
The Pit's away, but let me mak it clear
Ah don't begrudge a meenit o that year.

Friday 8 June, 1984
Brilliant sunshine today. Went up to swimming pool 11am and lay in sun till 2:30pm. There were two or three young miners in who said they had been to London yesterday. They said that they never saw any rioting.

Saturday 9 June, 1984
Another really sunny day. Lay in garden for a while. On the news they said there was a massive rally in Edinburgh for the Scottish Miners' Gala Day. The NUM said there was 100,000 people there; the media said 30,000. All the same, it seemed a successful day.

Thursday 14 June, 1984
The talks between the NCB and the Union collapsed today. The NCB saying more pits could close – with no redundancy payments. There must be a lot of worried miners, myself included, probably.

Saturday 16 June, 1984
A miner from Yorkshire, Joe Green, aged 55, was killed by a lorry on the picket line yesterday.

Monday 18 June, 1984
There was a major battle at Orgreave Coking Plant today. Very violent scenes, worst of the Strike so far. There were over 5,000 pickets and 3,000 police, some had travelled by bus from up here, and I saw a few local faces on telly. Arthur Scargill was knocked out by a riot shield, though police say he fell. It's a disgrace that the Government can ignore all this on one hand, and deviously engineer pay rises for other unions on the other.

Saturday 23 June, 1984
Received letter from Coal Board Chief Ian MacGregor today. It

was very vague and didn't really say anything of substance... so I wrote him one back. I don't suppose he'll receive it personally though.

Monday 25 June, 1984

58 miners arrested at Bilston Glen Colliery today. Some men were trying to work this week to qualify for their holiday pay. I can't say I blame them really. It's the Steel Union's conference this week, so they are trying to reach agreement on the amount of coke being used. The NUR have stepped up their backing for the miners, they intend to block all movement of fuel, and disrupt rail travel with days of action.

Helen Gray, Cumnock

At the stairt o the Strike ah worked pairt time
It wisnae easy, the weans wir juist wee
But ye took things then in yer stride, ye see
Ma man wis gaun oot oan the picket line.
The weemin aa goat theirsels organised
Makin meals, crèches fir watchin the weans
A bus ran tae London, we juist drew names
Ah goat tae go, which wis a nice surprise.
The bad times?, it broke some faimilies up
An the debt we goat intae wisnae real;
Cheap Cider an wine aye helped things tae heal,
A greet an a song, tae cheer wirsels up.
The papers an telly fed us pure shit...
But eftir the Strike we knew whit wis whit.

Thursday 28 June, 1984
Mum sent me up the town to buy some groceries. I asked for three sirloin steaks at the Co-operative, and a chap who must've been a miner said, 'Here's somebody who's not on Strike!' Afterwards I felt a bit embarrassed. Sometimes I should count my blessings really, even though I complain a lot, I should learn to shut my mouth. I don't suppose I've ever really known what hardship is. I'll need to pay Mum back somehow when this is all over. There was a big write-up about the Strike in the *Cumnock Chronicle* today. I'll have to cut it out and keep it.

Monday 16 June, 1984
High Court ruled against the Union ban at Cheltenham GCHQ, more pressure on the Government. The Docks Strike has been stepped up, no solution there either. The NCB and NUM meet again on Wednesday. There was some picket trouble at a power station in Wales today, nothing on the scale of Orgreave though.

Friday 20 July, 1984
As expected, all the Dockers went back to work today. The Government is stepping in on the Miners' Strike, I don't know whether that will help or not as Arthur Scargill is pledged to putting the Tories out of power. I lay in the back garden all day, it was gloriously sunny.

Sunday 22 July, 1984
Didn't get up till about 11am. Went out and polished the car, that took about an hour. Went up the town to see what was doing. Met Craig Murray, Tom Houston and Stewart Dickson outside Tally's Café. We decided to go for a run in the car, the four of us drove up Crawick, it was very sunny and warm. We stopped at a place where there was a lot of cars, I noticed at least half a dozen miners and their families, people who would usually have gone abroad for a holiday. We all stopped and went

swimming in the Burn for about half an hour. It was great, and quite warm. Got home about 4pm.

Monday 30 July, 1984
David Riddell phoned to say he and three of the boys were needing a lift from Glasgow, as they'd just arrived back from Ibiza. I agreed to go and pick them up. Got them at Buchanan Street Bus Station. On leaving Glasgow on M8 there was a huge articulated lorry in the middle of the road at the Eaglesham turn-off. I didn't realise what he was doing and I tried to ease past him on the left hand lane. Suddenly the lorry pulled in in front of me. I had no chance and the cab hit the car dead centre on the door pillar. I slewed over the road and the rear of the car hit a stationary Austin Maxi car. My car was a write-off. I'd only had it for a week and a half. [That's what I thought at the time, but it turned out it could be repaired.] The police arrived, and after taking the details from everyone they escorted us in the car (which was still driving) to the Mearns Autos Garage. We were all quite shocked. It's just typical that a disaster like this should happen at such a bad time.

Rab Gray, Cumnock

Ah'm wan o the lucky yins ah wid say
There's nuthin fir young yins aboot here noo
Ma middle boys scunnert, stuck oan the Broo
They talk o 'Long term prospects', whit are they?
It's aa Opencast wi their twelve hour shifts
The big boys hae goat the ba at their fit
Ye've twae choices, pal, 'Tak it or leave it!'
They don't waant ony unions causin rifts.
It's no the same as when the Pits wir gaun
Ah'd gae back doon ablow in a meenit
A different class o fowk, an ah mean it
A place ye'd nevvir tae ask fir a haun.
In this world noo they'd stab their ain brither
Doon there ye looked eftir yin anither.

21st Week of Strike

Saturday 4 August, 1984

At 11am I noticed a large crowd outside the community centre. Went along and there were about 50 to 80 policemen milling around. Seemingly, a local man, Hugh Robertson, had organised a meeting of workers to find out the general feeling of the men. The community centre was packed with men from Kirkconnel, Cumnock and Dalmellington there, but when Hugh Robertson got up to speak he was howled down by the militants, consisting of Barry McLatchie, Wullie McKnight and some of the hard core from Cumnock. There was a lot of ill-feeling and the meeting broke down in disarray about 11:15am. Men were shouting and bawling at each other. I was standing talking to Jim Stewart, who was with a bunch of the moderate men, as the Cumnock men came out of the Centre and got onto their bus they gave the guys I was with a lot of abuse and were writing 'Scabs' on the bus window. I realised I was standing with the wrong team, so I moved off and stood with the rest of the young men who were standing there, they asked why I was standing with the Scabs. After about 20 minutes the crowd and the police dispersed. I heard later that night that some of the miners who frequented the Bowling Green Club were going to boycott it if Barry McLatchie continued to sing there. There was even a phone call to say that the windows of the club would all be smashed in if he continued there. Later on I met Tom Park, a local Union guy, who told me that Arthur Scargill would be speaking in Cumnock on the 26th of August.

Monday 6 August, 1984

Dull, drizzly morning. Went picking mushrooms again in field across from the old sewerage on the Nith. Collected a big bag and will freeze them. There were a lot of pickets at Longannet Colliery today trying to stop a miner who had repeatedly tried to cross the picket line in his blue Bedford van. There were a lot of pickets arrested. There was also trouble at pits in South Wales and Merseyside.

Tuesday 7 August, 1984
There was more picket violence today as some men tried to go to work. Two Yorkshire miners are taking legal action through the High Court to try and force a National Ballot.

Wednesday 8 August, 1984
A crowd of miners had rioted today at a pit in England and smashed windows and damaged cars of men who had been working. The violence has been pretty bad this week, almost the worst of the 5 months old Strike.

Saturday 11 August, 1984
In the space of a fortnight I've lost my car, all my money, my job prospects look very bleak and have now split up with my girlfriend. Whoever made the prediction about the world ending in 1984 wasn't very far wrong.

Yvonne Hodge, Cumnock

Ah wis juist nine at the time o the Strike
Ah thocht it wis great cause we goat free meals
But money wis ticht, fowk suffert fir real
Ah wis juist a wean though, nevvir knew, like.
Ah couldnae unnerstaun, we'd nae new claes,
When ither yins wir getting new trainers,
Ah caa'd fowk 'Scab', but ye ken whit weans are
Like, ah regret some things ah used tae say.
Ah mind ma dad in the kitchen greetin
Ah asked 'Whit's wrang?', an he said they wir beat
Noo things are worse, an they nevvir wir great
It's aa chainged roond here since they goat beaten.
Ah'm nineteen noo wi a wean o ma ain
Ah've seen enough anger, seen enough pain.

Wednesday 15 August, 1984
Went up to swimming pool. Stayed there from 11am till 3:30pm. It was very sunny. There were large turnouts of pickets today, almost two or three thousand, at a pit in Yorkshire, as the first Yorkshire miner to break the Strike went back to work. They've also decided to close two production lines at Castlehill Mine in Fife, with the loss of probably two to three hundred jobs.

Thursday 16 August, 1984
There were thousands more pickets in action today as more men went back to work. The NCB said that due to the effects of the Strike more men's jobs could be at risk than in the original closure plan. Now that they can see a chink in the armour they're going to put the boot in. If the Strike collapses they'll close everything in sight, the Trade Union Movement and the Labour party will possibly never recover.

Monday 20 August, 1984
Really sunny again. Sunbathed in garden from 11:30am till about 4pm. The temperature was hitting the 80s today! There was a big picket at Gascoine Wood Colliery in Yorkshire today as a couple of miners tried to go to work. Went to brass band practice tonight. It was so hot we played outside. There's a threat of water rationing in Strathclyde in seven weeks unless there is some really heavy rain.

Tuesday 21 August, 1984
Gloriously sunny again today. Spent most of day changing engine on mini-van. John Gibson was helping me. It was hard work and we were out in the sun most of the day. There was some severe picket line violence at pits in England today. Barricades were set alight and police in riot gear were in action. Here, in New Cumnock, there were about 100 police on duty as Hugh Robertson (the man who held the 'Back to Work' meeting)

attempted to go to work. There must've been a hundred or more pickets running around and windows were smashed at Robertson's house. I heard later that three pickets, who boarded NCB buses and entered the Killoch Pit grounds, had been given their notice by management. There seem to be some disturbing undercurrents in this dispute raising their ugly heads at the moment. I can't really define the lines between good and bad anymore. I feel I should believe in the Union, but the media has twisted and distorted the issue out of proportion. But why do the TUC and the other Unions, and the Labour party, sit back for about 5 months and mouth off verbal support and do nothing to help the NUM?

Danny Gemmel, Auchinleck

Scargill said we'd be oot anither year
We wir rock bottom an morale wis low
Dae ah regret the Strike? Morally no
But that feenished maist o the boys in here.
The village noo?, nuthin but a ghaist toon
Nae future, nae joabs, auld men walkin dugs
Aa they leeve fir noo's their Buckie an drugs
Shops aa boarded up wi their signs torn doon.
Ma faimily wir aa fae mining stock
Faither, grandfaither, three generations
Hung oot tae dry bi the 'Wealth o Nations'
They talk o wastage, but they're wastin fowk.
They've spent mair keeping miners oan the dole
Wid it no be cheaper tae dig fir coal?

Wednesday 22 August, 1984
More trouble up the town this morning. Hughie Robertson went to work again. There was a large police and picket presence. I heard that a bus drew into Danny Rae's Transport Café and soldiers changed into police uniforms. The bus used to pick Hughie up was covered in paint by the pickets, who then emptied all the black bin liners all over the road. In Cumnock later in the day I saw the pit bus on its way to New Cumnock (still covered in paint). It was escorted by two police vans and two police cars. On way home from group practice tonight there was a large contingent of pickets outside the Killoch, and a police car as well. There were two buses sitting and one looked as though the windows were smashed in, but I'm not really sure about that yet? On the national news there was severe rioting by pickets in England, especially in Yorkshire, where police had riot gear on.

Thursday 23 August, 1984
The Dockers in Scotland have called all their men out because the ISTC (Iron and Steel Trades Confederation) have begun unloading the coal ship from Poland at the Hunterston power station terminal. There is a strong likelihood that another National Dock Strike will begin tomorrow. There were five vans of police to escort Hughie Robertson to his work this morning.

Friday 24 August 1984
Heard that some pickets had laid out car tyres across the Nith Bridge this morning and set them on fire in an attempt to stop Hughie Robertson going to his work. The Dock Strike has become national as of this morning.

Monday 27 August, 1984
Met Ewing Hope (Scottish NUM youth delegate) he said there had been a large crowd at Cumnock yesterday for Arthur

Scargill's visit. Ewing is very militant in his outlook and was broadcasting today on *Westsound Radio News*. He said his wife and family had received threatening phone calls because of his pro-Strike views. By contrast, there was a very good article in the *Daily Record* today by Jimmy Reid, condemning Scargill's actions and pointing out the damage being caused to the Trade Union Movement. At the end of the day there'll be no winners really. A Drongan butcher who'd been giving 'tick' to his customers (striking miners) amounting to c. £3,000, had his windows put in when he stopped giving it. The Dockers meet again tomorrow, but a big majority of them are continuing to work.

Tuesday 28 August, 1984
The Dockers are split on whether to Strike or not. There were three pickets arrested in New Cumnock today. The car taking Hughie Robertson to work had its windscreen smashed. A Strike-breaker from Mauchline had his car overturned by pickets, he later appeared on the *Scottish News*. Margaret Thatcher held a committee meeting today to discuss the situation, but I can't see any change in her attitude. The TUC meets next week, and the Dockers will hold more meetings later in the week.

Archie Campbell, Kelty

Ah'm sixty-nine, ah'd aye worked doon the Pits
We'd seeven or eicht Pits roond aboot here
An ah've worked in six o them owre the years
But ah'm gled noo that ah've hung up ma buits.
Ah focht the closures in the early days
Ah'll admit though it nevvir duin much guid
Labour shut as mony as Thatcher did.
During eichty-fowr ma knees wir away
Ah wis oan insurance richt through the Strike
Which wis probably juist as weel fir me
Ah could nevvir keep ma gub shut ye see.
We'd nae real hardship cause the wife worked like
The young yins aa peyed digs, but here's the rub
Hauf it's aye mooched back when ah'm doon the pub.

Wednesday 29 August, 1984
There were 87 arrested for picketing Hughie Robertson's house in Farden Avenue today. They were all taken to Ayr Police Station. It's frightening to realise that the violence has arrived on our very doorsteps. New Cumnock was mentioned in the national headlines tonight.

25th Week of Strike

Monday 3 September, 1984
The TUC Conference began today. Arthur Scargill gave a rousing speech asking for more support for the miners. There were about two and a half thousand supporters outside the hall, and just as many police, but things remained quite orderly though. The TUC pledged to support the miners, but there were some dissenters, notably the Electricians' Union, the Steel Union and the Engineers' Union.

Thursday 6 September, 1984
The NCB and NUM are still haggling over whether there will be talks on Sunday or not. There was mass violence at Kellingley Colliery in Yorkshire today between 3,000 pickets and about the same number of police, many of them in riot gear.

Friday 7 September, 1984
The DHSS were handing out money to the married men today at the community centre. The talks are still on on Sunday, but I'm not too hopeful about a settlement.

Monday 10 September, 1984
The talks between NCB and NUM have continued at a hotel in Edinburgh all day, but there is no sign of any progress yet. Hopefully there may be some news tomorrow.

Tuesday 11 September, 1984
Went up to the Strike Centre about 1:30pm, there were a few miners hanging about, everyone was pretty fed up, the talks weren't making much headway today, no-one is very optimistic. Ian MacGregor and Ned Smith flew off back to London. It looks as though there's some sneaky negotiations with the Government taking place. If they have reached some form of compromise it wouldn't surprise me if Mrs Thatcher snubbed it out.

Andrew Leys, Whitburn

The Strike wis a laugh, a brilliant laugh
We hud some funny times doun South, aa they
Wee characters ye met, the things they'd dae
That boy killt in Wales though, that wis plain daft.
Polkemmet, aye, weel, that wis juist a crime
They deliberately flooded the pit
Withdrew the safety cover, that wis it
Destroyed oor joabs, Christ, they should hae duin time.
Ah taen ma 'Dundy' an twelve weeks in lieu
Ah splashed oot a bit, bocht a brand new bike
Ah gie it an airing (wance a year like!)
Ah'd some tough times tae, spent time oan the Buroo
Ah've struggled at times tae buy the weans shoes
But we nevvir stairved then, we'll no stairve nou.

Thursday 13 September, 1984
The talks are making some progress, but have been adjourned till tomorrow. The Dockers talks broke down. NACODS (National Association of Colliery Oversmen, Deputies and Shotfirers) are threatening to come out in sympathy with the miners. The financial editor of the *Times* was on telly, he reckons a settlement will take some time yet.

Friday 14 September, 1984
We heard on the news today that the latest talks have collapsed after 30 hours of meetings. I felt really sick. It seems that every time I build up my hopes up they are dashed to the ground again. As predicted by the *Times* editor it looks as though Scargill is going for broke and calling on the TUC to give concrete backing to the Strike. It's as though we were climbing a summit and every time it looked as though we were nearing the top, another peak appears. Some families must be in a desperate situation with mounting debts and rent arrears. It has been six months now, if I can come through this and survive then I think I'll be able to cope with anything.

Saturday 17 September, 1984
The NUM have agreed to a third party mediating in the Strike, but the Electricians' Union are not very forthcoming in giving anything but verbal support. Mum overheard a young woman, with two kids about 5 and 3, saying it was hard trying to explain to the kids that there wouldn't be much for them at Christmas. That's the human aspect of the Strike I suppose?

Sunday 30 September, 1984
Still no real moves in the Pit Strike. We'll probably find out this week if the NACODS men are coming out, they voted overwhelmingly for Strike action. The High Court has ruled that the Strike is illegal in Yorkshire and Derbyshire and the

press said that the majority of miners would go back to work tomorrow, that's a real load of shit if ever I heard any. It's strange but I think that any of the ordinary working lads can sense when there is any real positive move, and then something happens.

30th Week of Strike

Monday 8 October, 1984
The Strike is still dragging on. The High Court still hasn't jailed Arthur Scargill, and the Tory press are still screaming for his blood as usual. There's talk of taxes (VAT probably) going up (Advisory, Conciliation and Arbitration Service) to pay for the Strike. The NACODS men have met with ACAS, as have the NCB, but nothing has come of these meetings yet. I must resign myself to the fact that we'll probably be out till Christmas now. The bitter feeling remains that the other Unions and the Labour party are doing nothing to help us really. I'm coping not too badly at the moment, financially I'll probably manage to tick over if I keep to a strict budget.

Mick McGahey, Penicuik

We aa thocht that Thatcher wis backing doon
But naw, she wis only bidin her time
While Ridley wis planning tae shut each mine
She wis makin shair we'd dance tae her tune.
Ah wis arrested nine times in the Strike
They sackt me fir that, it's whit ye expect
If ye're political ye're aye suspect
Undesirable, an they'll get ye like.
Then ah dodged away oan joab creation
Ah enjoyed it, it goat me fit again
Climbin hills, wi bags o trees, in the rain
Ah eked it oot oan the compensation.
Ah work as a hospital porter noo
Ah feel quite lucky, joabs roond here are few.

Wednesday 10 October, 1984
Arthur Scargill was fined £1,000 by the High Court today. The NUM was fined £200,000.

Thursday 11 October, 1984
The NUM are still meeting with ACAS, but I can't see any progress being made really. John Nairn, who's WPIS (Weekly Paid Industrial Staff) at Barony says the pickets tried to stop the Deputies from going in to their work, this brings the fear that the NCB will use this as an excuse to pull the plug on the pit, and we could all end up out of work with no redundancy money. I don't think this would come as a great surprise though.

Wednesday 17 October, 1984
The news was all about the Strike again. The NACODS men are coming out on Strike next Thursday. There's more talk of power cuts. This has been the most decisive move for a while. The pound dropped to a new low ($1:20) and the FT Index dropped an incredible 29 points.

Wednesday 24 October, 1984
The NACODS men met with NCB and ACAS today and came to an agreement, so their Strike, planned for tomorrow, has been called off. The NUM meets with the NCB tomorrow.

Thursday 25 October, 1984
The High Court has ordered the sequestration of all the NUM's funds. Typical of them. They were shitting themselves yesterday because of the threatened NACODS Strike, and now that it's called off they're putting the boot in.

Monday 29 October, 1984
The news was on about Scargill's connection with Libya. They're obviously trying to trump up some exaggerated charge against

the NUM. They're meeting again with ACAS on Wednesday, but it's now quite plain that nothing will come of those talks.

34th Week of Strike

Friday 2 November, 1984
Went to funeral up Afton Cemetery today. The graveyard overlooks the opencast mine and above the service the interminable grind and squeal of earthmoving machinery could be heard. The NCB have offered the miners a bonus Christmas pay of around £600, if they work a complete month from November the 19th. More blatant bribery, though God knows some men must be on the verge of financial ruin, and this could be the Carrot on the stick to get them back to work.

Joe Owens, Blackburn

Ah stairted in Riddochill Colliery
Forty-six year later in Bilston Glen
Ah taen ma 'dundy', an that wis the end
Bi then it wis aamaist arbitrary.
Ah wis seeckened wi aa their dirty tricks
Bankrupt the country tae beat the miners
Some wir heroes tae Tory hardliners
That guy at Polkemmet wha pued the switch
The Coal Board hud the gall tae promote him
Millions o pounds worth o plant wir destroyed
The kind o sabotage Hitler enjoyed
If they'd gien me a gun ah'd hae shot him.
We wir unner extreme Capitalism,
It wisnae a time fir Idealism.

Monday 5 November, 1984
A lot of miners turned out for work today. They can't be blamed really as the NCB is offering some big Christmas bonuses to get them back. Neil Kinnock, the Labour leader has refused to appear at Miners' Rallies, and the NUM's funds, £8 million, have been sequestrated in Ireland.

Wednesday 7 November, 1984
The NCB say more men have turned up for work and there was some clashes between pickets and police in Yorkshire, mostly at Markham Colliery.

Friday 9 November, 1984
Sam phoned from Bridgend Pub and said the miners were being paid out, so I went to the community centre again. There was a queue of about a hundred men. The single men got paid out first, we all got £40 each. I'll just give the money to Mum.

Saturday 10 November, 1984
Heard there's to be a meeting of miners at Coach House Hotel tomorrow, to rally support for a return to work. It looks as though the Strike may be crumbling. I never imagined it could turn out this way. Unless there is some kind of miraculous turnaround by the other Unions, the TUC and the Labour party, then it looks as though the Strike may be finished. Mrs Pink (Coach House owner) won't be doing herself any favours tomorrow though, there could be some ugly scenes up the town.

Sunday 11 November, 1984
Went to play with brass band at Remembrance Service at Sanquhar. We paraded with the band from the Church to the Cenotaph. We played a couple of hymns, then Bobby Sanderson and I played the 'Last Post'. We then marched back to the Church for the Service, it was a cold, blustery day, but at least

it didn't rain. We played the hymns at the service, the Minister's service went on for a while, we finished about 12:30pm.

Monday 12 November, 1984

Mum woke me about 10am. Had to sign cheque for her that I'd received from Strike Welfare Fund. Went to Doctors this afternoon and had my ear syringed, it had been blocked all week. Dr MacSween went on about the Miners' Strike, he seems to have rather a Tory attitude towards things. He told me his daughter Ann is now doing a PhD at Leeds. Visited Chris Rollie at Auchinleck. We sat and talked for a while, mostly about the Strike. I think we both agree that if the miners can hold out till after Christmas then they might win. There were two or three men from New Cumnock went back to work today, but I'll have to wait and see whether more go back this week. The news went on about the severe rioting in Yorkshire and the NCB said more and more men were returning to work.

Jackie Aitchison, Dalkeith

Ah wis born at 'The bottom o the bing',
An went intae the Pits in sixty-nine
Ma interest in the union grew owre time
Ah wis made Branch Secretary, that's something
Ah'll aye be prood o. Then we hud the Strike.
The NCB targeted Bilston Glen
An did aa that they could tae brek the men
They'd gae sneakin roond mens doors late at night
Bribing, cajoling them tae go back in
They painted a 'Border' ootside the Mine
Ah goat sacked fir daurin tae cross their line
We focht a tribunal, but couldnae win.
Ah'm back oan ma feet, but its cost me dear
Eftir it ah wis blacklisted fir years.

Pat Rattray, Kelty

Ah leeve in a place in Fife caa'd Kelty
It wis built oan coal, but there's nae Pits noo
An men that's goat work traivel, baur a few
We saw it comin ah could hae telt ye.
Ah picketed Longannet, Castlehill,
Solsgirth, Kincardine, ah wis at Orgreave
They jiled me twice, ye'd haurdly believe
Ah'd nevvir yince been in ony trouble.
In ninety-twa we aa walked tae London
Whit a fantastic adventure that wis
Ye'd ne'er believe, fowk waanted tae touch us
An the kindness we goat fae everyone.
Naw, ah've nae regrets, ah focht the guid fight
An did it because ah thocht it wis right.

Thursday 15 November, 1984
There were some windows smashed in New Cumnock last night. Sandy McGhee, who'd returned to work, got his windows broken and Tam Park, the Union man, had his windows broken too. There was an STV film unit at the community centre, and on the main news, Alex Montgomery, the New Cumnock Strike Leader, put the case that the Strike was still solid, but I've heard there are a lot of men who are on the verge of returning to work. I'm still sitting on the fence. I think it will take a major return to work though before I go back.

Tuesday 20 November, 1984
A chap was killed at Auchinleck today while digging coal from an embankment. His name was Gorman and he worked at Barony, though I can't recall him, and he did work on the Surface.

Wednesday 21 November, 1984
Mum and Sam are busy making Holly wreaths at the moment for Christmas. A letter from the NCB had arrived asking me to sign a form saying I would be willing to return to work if there were sufficient men who would return together. I haven't really considered what to do about it yet. Do I sign and probably admit the Strike is beaten, or do I ignore it and wait and see what the Majority decide to do? It's quite a dilemma really.

Friday 23 November, 1984
Got up 10am. Delivered wreaths for the Gorman funeral at Auchinleck, then picked up my suit from dry cleaners at Cumnock. It cost £3:50. Called in at Alex Jess's for a while. We discussed the Strike. He told me he overheard some old men on a Public Bench discussing the Strike. Seemingly one of them didn't have much to say on the subject, and when he got up and left one old boy said to the other, 'Honey wouldn't have much to say...

he was a Scab during the last Strike.' These men were about 70 years old, and they were talking about the General Strike in 1926! This emphasises the bitter divisions between working men and how long they last. More local men are returning to work. My mate John Barbour returned to work on Monday, he says he doesn't care what people think. I can't imagine he'll be very popular with the boys at the Strike Centre. The Strike looks as though an imminent collapse is due, there doesn't seem to be any silver lining on the horizon now.

Billy McLean, Kelty

Ah kent eftir the Strike that we wir beat
This manager ah'd hud a run-in wae
Said (three weeks eftir the Strike bi the way)
'It's constant nichts or there's the fuckin gate!'
Naebody will ken the true cost o the Strike
Truth is the Tories juist waanted revenge
McGreegor an Maggie oot tae avenge
Theirsels fir the seeventies an that, like.
Stories ah could tell; Orgreave picket line
Led us straicht in, they aa kent whit tae dae
They battered the fuck oot o us aa day
An the News that wis shown wis redesigned
They werenae the true facts, that wisnae real
'Truth' wis whit ma country tried tae conceal.

Sunday 25 November, 1984

We left for the Blantyre gig with the Group at 6pm. Got there about 8pm as Ian McEwan, our singer, was late. Played very boring gig to a bunch of very boring people. Ian had a bit to drink, but said he'd drive us home. There were five of us in Ian's old Ford Cortina estate car. We pulled in at a petrol station in East Kilbride, and there was a police patrol car sitting there. Whilst in the shop there the two policemen came in and Ian began mouthing off at them. He told them he was a miner (which he wasn't) then they told us to shut up and move on. They took the number of our car, obviously thinking we were a bunch of pickets, thanks to Ian. John Harris took the car keys off Ian and now drove. Ian sat in rear with me & Billy. The police followed us out onto the road, Ian was giving them the Fingers, then once we were out of town a bit they flagged our car down. The two policemen got out, Ian shouted, 'What's this? The Flying Squad?' Then another squad car pulled up and four policemen grabbed Ian quite roughly, one of them having already produced a set of handcuffs. They then cuffed him and said they were charging him with Breach of the Peace. By this time there were about 8 policemen, then a van and an Inspector arrived. All the while they had thought we were pickets, and they asked us which pit we were going to. Billy explained that we were a musical group, on our way home from a gig. The policemen looked unbelievingly at us, then Billy lifted the tailgate of the Cortina to reveal our white suits and two guitar cases. The police looked at each other again, and realised that we were not pickets after all, and after a lot of questions they hauled Ian away to the cells. We quickly went on our way, passing yet another police van down the road a bit. I must admit I was very scared. I *was* a striking miner, and if we had been pickets we'd all have been arrested for certain, after seeing the vans and the treatment that Ian received.

Monday 26 November, 1984
Lot of talk in the Papers today, and all weekend, about the picket violence. A miner in Yorkshire (Castleford) had his house burnt down, and two miners were severely beaten by gangs breaking into their homes. For the first time, Arthur Scargill has condemned this violence. The TGWU (Transport and General Workers Union) were fined £200,000 for Contempt today over the Austin Rover Strike, still remains to be seen whether they will pay up or not. There seems to be 80 men working at Barony and almost 200 at Killoch. Already the Government and the NCB are hinting at going back on their word about Compulsory Redundancies, which was wholly expected I suppose.

Wednesday 28 November, 1984
The TUC met to try and get peace talks in the Strike going again. Mick McGahey was served a writ today and the NUM's money in Luxembourg has been sequestrated.

Sunday 2 December, 1984
Heard there had been quite a riot at the Kello Rovers Club in Kirkconnel last night. Some guys I know from Barony were there, Danny and Bert Black, a big fight had started and there were about 10 policemen involved and around 20 arrests were made. They say there was blood all over the place and tables and chairs got broken. In the news, the miners' leaders have had the right to manage the NUM funds taken off them by the High Court, so they are meeting today to discuss whether they should abide by the High Court ruling.

John McCormack, Fallin

(i)

Ah left schule at fifteen, oan a Friday
Nae exams then or ony palaver
If the surface Foreman kent yer faither
That wis it. Ah stairted oan the Monday.
Fallin hus ayeways been a village Pit
Here, in the village, Polmaise Three and Four
A tunnel linking up, faur doun ablow,
Polmaise One and Two, doun the road a bit.
Fir fowr or five year ah duin surface work
Then oncost joabs till ah duin ma trainin
Then constant backshift cause ah wis playin
Fitba at weekends, signed up wi Falkirk.
Ah played professional fir eicht seasons –
When we won the Cup in fifty-seeven.

38th Week of Strike

Monday 3 December, 1984
A fellow Rafferty from Kirkconnel was severely beaten up today for returning to his work at Killoch Colliery. The NUM have decided to continue defying the High Court, the sequestrator is having trouble getting the money out of Luxembourg.

Thursday 13 December, 1984
Rehearsed with the Group today. We learned the Wham Xmas number and went through our Xmas medley again. It was very cold at the practice and I was glad to get home. Arthur Scargill was in court today over violence at Orgreave, and members of TUC are meeting with NCB tomorrow.

Friday 14 December, 1984
Arthur Scargill was fined £250 for obstruction today. The talks between TUC and the Government came to nothing, as expected.

Monday 17 December, 1984
Tam Park, the Union Secretary, flagged me down and gave me a cheque from CISWO (Coal Industry Social Welfare Organisation) for £5. Nothing happening on Strike front at moment, the TUC still not coming forth with support.

Saturday 22 December, 1984
The news had pictures of pickets and police singing Christmas carols on the picket line. All good stuff for the Country's Morale and the Christmas Cheer!

43rd Week of Strike

Wednesday 2 January, 1985
On the news, the Strike is still entrenched, the Coal Board says

more men are back at their work, the Board are making a big push in the papers saying they'll give all the miners £1,000 tax free in their first month back at work.

John McCormack, Fallin

(ii)

In thae days we'd aa come hame frae the Pit
In wir workin claes, an yer een wir black
We'd stoap at the Welfare tae hear the crack
An each wan o us still hud oan wir buits.
The place ah worked wis a faur-away run
We'd focht the Germans, an the joke goat told
That nou we wir tryin tae steal their coal
We'd a fowr mile hike, it wisnae much fun.
Wir jaikets wir aff, the tap o the brae
Stripped doun tae wir trousers, buits an kneepads
Ah'm telling ye frien, the heat wis that bad
Extra waater goat sent doun every day.
Ah grew richt scunnert round about that time
Nearly jined the Airmy tae quit the mine.

Monday 7 January, 1985
The NCB claiming there were 1,000 men back at work, though the NUM disputed this. Nine men were jailed for setting fire to Scab buses last year. They got two and a half years each. Local MP George Foulkes was on the picket line at Killoch today, as more men went back to work the national papers carry full page ads trying to persuade men to go back to work. There's still 140,000 men on Strike and it will drag on until there is some kind of 'negotiated settlement'.

Saturday 12 January, 1985
Played Mauchline Club, it was quite busy. Managed to get a booking from them for next Friday as one we had at Annan got cancelled. A lot of the clubs are feeling the pinch from the Strike, and we've got quite a few cancellations. It'll be quite a lean time through January to March.

Monday 14 January, 1985
The news said a lot more men had returned to work today, there were 90 men at Killoch, and about 30 at Barony. I'm still holding out, though I don't really know why anymore. Nottingham and South Derby are forming a breakaway union from the NUM. So it looks as though the Government have succeeded in splitting the workers down the middle after all. I say I won't go back because I won't travel on a bus with meshing on the windows, but maybe that's an excuse I make for myself, I don't know. I don't think I've ever found it easy to admit defeat.

Tuesday 15 January, 1985
Some arrests at Killoch today. The news and media report quite a large return to work. There's been heavy snowfall in South of England over the last few days and Europe is having the worst winter in years, it being minus 10 degrees in Italy. We've

escaped lightly so far, but the forecast is for the snow to hit us, probably tomorrow.

Tuesday 22 January, 1985
Went down to Cumnock as there was a SCEBTA (Scottish Colliery Enginemen, Boilermen and Tradesmen's Association) meeting at the Town Hall. All the Barony tradesmen were there, about 80 in all. I think about 10 must be back at work. They discussed the fact that the management had turned down the safety cover provided by the Union throughout the dispute. They were saying they had enough men working permanently to cover the work. A few of the men were very much afraid that they might have broken service if they stay out for more than a year, and this was making a few of them contemplate going back to work. The three winding engine men are faced with the threat that someone else will be trained for their job, so they said they would return to work on 4 February. Jim Murray, who's around 50, voiced the opinion that he'd followed the Union faithfully for about 11 months and now he felt we were getting nowhere and the Union was being split down the middle, and he was going to return to work. He didn't really get much support, though a lot of the men must be thinking along the same lines. The meeting adjourned with the decision to place a formal complaint in front of the management, and we all agreed to meet again next Tuesday.

John McCormack, Fallin

(iii)

Ah became the union delegate
At the schule ah aye liked tae see fair play
Ah feel the same wey tae this very day
Held the post till they pit me out the gate.
We'd hit this fault, afore the Miners' Strike
We said we'd drive through it tae hit the coal
But Wheeler juist waantit us oan the dole
Even though we turned doon our bonus, like,
The men wir desprait fir the place tae go
In June eichty-three things came tae a peak
He locked aa the miners out fir five weeks
We won a tribunal though, and our dough
Five weeks back-pey wis peyed out in our haun
Wheeler wis not a very happy man.

Sunday 27 January, 1985
The Sunday papers were full of the Government demanding a surrender from Arthur Scargill, wanting him to agree to the pit closures.

Monday 28 January, 1985
Watched the news. The return to work was only half of last week's total, dropping from 1,800 to 800. I suppose everyone is pinning their hopes on tomorrow's talks.

Tuesday 29 January, 1985
The coal talks don't seem to have achieved much today. The NCB still looking for a written agreement on pit closures. The pound was still taking a battering, bank rates went up 2%. Went to the SCEBTA meeting at Cumnock Town Hall. Morale was a bit better this week because of the talks. Dougie Aitken (Union Rep) got a bit of a ribbing because of his holiday in Tenerife. There were about 70 men there, we heard that the management were training people up for other people's jobs, and that some men who weren't qualified were being given written dispensations from the management to carry out inspections. The tradesmen are still solid though and we all agreed to meet a fortnight from tonight. I felt quite proud tonight as I left the meeting.

Wednesday 30 January, 1985
The talks have predictably broken down again, the NCB still wanting a written agreement on pit closures. There was a mass picket at Barony, a lot of men down from Fife.

Thursday 31 January, 1985
Arthur Scargill was on the news with Michael Eaton discussing the reasons for the talks breaking down. I received a cheque for £15 from the Strike Relief Fund today.

48th Week of Strike

Wednesday 6 February, 1985

The Strike's still deadlocked this week. Quite a few more have went back to work, there was a row in the House of Commons when Thatcher was accused of prolonging the Strike, and NACODS are worried that the NCB might backpedal on their deal, though the Government and the NCB both strenuously deny this. Frances Colliery in Fife has been closed with the loss of about 500 jobs, everyone's blaming each other as usual. There was a Union meeting at Cumnock Town Hall tonight, but I never went.

John McCormack, Fallin

(iv)

Within fowr weeks the fault hud been driven
Hit coal that wis six feet high all the way
But three hunner men wir peyed aff next day
Depriving aa they men o a living.
An act o industrial villainy
Wi nae thocht fir Fallin they shut the Pit
A place wi twenty years work left in it
They needed the money fir the Barony.
We met in the Welfare, made out a list
The managers oaffice wis ma next stop
He said 'You're fir the big ship lollipop!'
He meant ah wis out, an widnae be missed.
George Bolton said 'Sort it out fir yersel'
The show wis by, ah should hae kent masel.

Thursday 7 February, 1985
The NCB say there'll be no new talks on the Strike, but the NACODS men are still unhappy with their deal. Heard through the grapevine that the tradesman are going back to work on Monday, will have to wait and see though. Got £5 from the Strike Fund.

Friday 8 February, 1985
The news states that over 8,000 men had went back to work this week. The biggest return of the Strike. Spoke to a couple of local lads, they said they'll probably go back to work next week. It's bitterly cold with an icy wind, there was heavy snow in Ireland and in Wales.

Sunday 10 February, 1985
The South Wales miners are having a vote on Wednesday to return to work. There's been really heavy snow in England throughout the week, but we've had hardly any snow up here in Scotland, compared to what we had last year.

Sunday 17 February, 1985
Had a pint in the Glendyne at Sanquhar. Met George Wallace from Kirkconnel, who I'd worked on pit-head with, he'd had a bit to drink, said he's back at work. Called in at Rab Rorison's, talked for a while, he's back at his work as well. He says there's a lot of ill-feeling between the men who went back at say Christmas, and the men who went back earlier. The talks broke down again today. The NCB are refusing the TUC's latest proposals.

Monday 18 February, 1985
The news said the Prime Minister would meet the TUC on Thursday, but it looks like more Morale Breaking to me. Arthur Scargill was on, saying he would never sell out on his members.

I delivered a flower order to the housing scheme and met Joe Fulton at a bus stop. Joe was going back to his work, this was his first shift. Joe had always been a solid supporter of the Strike. He said there were only a handful of tradesmen still out on Strike. He looked a sad, desolate figure, standing in the biting cold wind by himself. If I don't go back to work this week then I suppose I'll definitely be back next week. They said 800 returned today. Went to brass band practice this evening, it was a hard blow again.

John McCormack, Fallin

(v)

Eftir the Strike ah wis loast fir a while
Nou ah fill forms in fir boys oan the dole
Help widows wi pensions claim fir their coal
Ye'll still see me gaun through Falkirks turnstiles
Ma playins aa duin fae the terracings nou
Ah went up tae Timex tae check the facts
Nevvir said ah'm a miner, if they ask
Ah say ah'm fae Stirling, juist passin through.
Ah feel different nou, lik ah've loast something
Cannae pit ma finger oan whit it is
Ah think it's the Pit that ah really miss
An memories o it aye seem tae bring
A burst o laughter frae the guid auld days
An sadness an anger aa fade away.

Tuesday 19 February, 1985
Took Margaret home at 12pm. The roads were treacherous with
black ice. Approaching the bad double bend at Polneul, I lost
control of the car, it spun off the road and smashed into a dry
stone wall. We were all right, but the car's written off again. I
felt sick. The police arrived and took all the details. Left the car
there and they gave us a lift into Sanquhar. Her Mum and Dad
got up and we had some tea. Spent night there.

Wednesday 20 February, 1985
After all my problems I'm back at square one again. Phoned
John Harris and he gave me a lift down to Henderson's Insurance
office, filled in claims form, I suppose it isn't so bad this time as
I'm insured fully comprehensive. Sent my road tax to Swansea
for refund. June Blackwood at the insurance office doesn't
seem too pleased, my insurance will probably go up again, but
she says they'll probably settle in two or three weeks. Phoned
my workmate John Gibson, he's went back to work today. He
phoned me when he got in, he says he's glad he's back, he got
two rest days to make up his first week, giving him a full pay
next week. So, I made the decision to go back to work. After
11 months, and now having no car, I'm beaten. Phoned the pit.
The time keeper, Andrew McKnight, said to start tomorrow.
Surprisingly, it wasn't a difficult phone call to make, and it was
one of the most momentous of my life. It'll be murder getting
up at 5am tomorrow. I don't know how other people will react
who are still on Strike, but I'll just have to face that, it's a very
strange feeling. I suppose I'll feel better when my first shift's in.

Thursday 21 February, 1985
Got up 5am. Walked up town to Lime Road to get bus. It
arrived at 5:40am. It was a Parks of Hamilton bus, with all the
windows caged off. I'd vowed not to travel on one, and here I
was climbing aboard. I still think it's very degrading. My clothes

were still in my locker at the baths from 11 months ago. I was handed my tokens at the Time Hall. Sat and talked to a lot of the tradesmen before going up to the Car Hall. There's only about 100 men left to come back to work out of a workforce of about 650. Spent surprisingly normal day at work, business as usual, there had been about 30 pickets shouting at the main gate as we came into work. Put in for three rest days, so that will give me a full week's pay next week. Went home on the Kirkconnel bus, which is a double-decker Parks bus, it dropped me off at the door. Went to bed for three hours, felt quite tired. The Government has now refused to hold any more talks at all on the Strike. These last few weeks have all been about Psychological Morale Breaking, and it has worked, and no-one can do anything about it. The South Wales miners are still solid, but they say they don't know how much longer they can support the Strike. John Harris picked me up for the Pavilion gig tonight, will have to travel in his car until mine is sorted out by the insurance.

Reprise: Big Wull

Drivin aff the nicht shifts ah'd see Big Wull,
Talkin tae hissel et the Tally's shop,
Dressed lik a hawker wha's een begged fir hope,
Waitin oan the bus tae cam owre the hill,
But they buses dinnae stoap there ony mair.
Then, ah thocht o Wull staunin, years ago,
Clean-cut, straicht an tidy, his een aglow,
Aye first wi the crack, a joke or a tear,
Noo he's nevvir shaved, an his mad een stare.
Ah've mind the men in his squad doon the pit,
Hou, eftir thir piece, in seelence they'd sit,
Lamps switcht aff, in the howe-dumb-deid; ah'm shair
They're maistly aa gaen, or else oan the dole,
Casualties tint in the war fir coal.

Friday 22 February, 1985
Got up 6am. Got Kirkconnel bus at 6:15am. Spent normal day at work, there's not much to do there at the moment, and the management seem to be very lax in discipline compared to what it used to be like. I just hung about the Car Hall all day and nobody really bothered with me. There's no Union as such at the pit just now but there is a workers committee which was formed to liaise between the men and the management. It's led by one of the men who came from Cardowan Pit. He had his clothes burnt off him in the Explosion there. Hughie Allan says the fellow was offered £12,000 compensation, but he expects to get more than that. Got home at 3pm. Slept for couple of hours. John Harris picked me up for Mossblown gig. Home from gig at 1am. I thought I would have felt worse about starting work, but funnily once you're there it seems the natural thing to do. Like everyone else, I just wish things were back to normal.

Monday 25 February, 1985
Struggled to get up 6am. Didn't get home from Dumfries gig last night till 2am and was still drunk when I got up. Quite a few new starts at work today. Not many pickets out today at the pit gates. Stories filtered in all day about men returning to work in Yorkshire and Wales. Was ill all day because of the drink last night, felt terrible, it's been a really long time since I'd gone to work in a state like that. Didn't go to brass band practice. Went to bed, was really shattered. Got up for few hours at 8pm. Pound dropped against the Dollar today, and the NCB claimed the biggest return to work on a Monday since the Strike began. Went to bed 10pm.

Tuesday 26 February, 1985
Felt a lot better today, finally recovered from Sunday night. Had quite a lot of work to do at pit today; had to change large air cylinder for mine car squeezer on Pit Bottom, it was

a heavy, dirty job. The deputy chief engineer, Alex Peters, says we might not be due any holidays this summer as we're only due a week's holiday pay. Paid £100 into bank today. Called in at Henderson's Insurance, got uneconomic repair notice for them from McGarva's Garage. More than 1,000 more miners returned to work today, though Arthur Scargill was still asking the men to stand firm. I don't seem to care much anymore, but that's not the whole feeling, it's a kind of resigned despair at the hopelessness of it all. Maybe when people realise that they've been told packs of lies and have been sold down the river, then the working people will stick together, but then again people have been saying this throughout history, I went back to work for the money.

Wednesday 27 February, 1985
Got up 6am. Bus picked me up 6:15am. There were only a handful of pickets at the pit gate. The majority of them came in a blue minibus from Netherthird. Run of the mill day at work. Built a cage shuttle for the winding cages. Hughie Allan was on about his claim for compensation for an accident at work. He's been fighting it for about two and a half years now! The Coal Board said they now have 50 per cent of the workforce working. I think they must be right. There was supposed to be a mass picket at Barony today, but it never materialised.

Thursday 28 February, 1985
Run of the mill day at work, nothing much happening. Was picked up by John Harris at 2:30pm and drove through the pickets in his car. They were all shouting. John and Billy thought it was a laugh. It was quite a warm, sunny day, people were playing football with their shirts off down on the beach. It's exceptionally mild for the time of year, we've had a really mild winter with hardly a drop of snow. The group practice went okay. Got home at 6pm. Taped *Top of the Pops*, then left for

'Grab-a-Granny' at Ayr Pavilion. It was mobbed. There were hundreds of Welsh guys up for the Scotland-Wales Rugby Match this Saturday. Got home at 2am. Got first pay today since I went on Strike 11 months ago, £106.

51st Week of Strike

Friday 1 March, 1985
Good old Friday. Only back at work a week and I'm glad it's Friday. Weren't many pickets today, about 25, saw Big Rusty Anderson and Harry Parker from Netherthird on picket line. On the news it said about 5,500 men had returned to work this week. The Wales and Durham Areas seem to be wanting an orderly return to work without a settlement. Arthur Scargill was on the telly, there's to be a special Delegate Conference on Sunday, and everyone expects there'll be a return to work on Monday. Mick McGahey was on telly as well, informing the Scottish miners to return to work. They had the look of two defeated men. Played Annan tonight. At the gig the PA gear developed a major electrical fault that blew up the mixing desk and my amp. We had to play gig with a makeshift PA. Had Indian meal on way home. Got home about 3am.

Sunday 3 March, 1985
Didn't get in till about 3am last night so stayed in bed till 12 noon. Watched current affairs programme *This Week, Next Week* with David Dimbleby. They were discussing the National Delegate Meeting in London of the NUM, to decide the Strike. They met in London from 12 till about 3pm. Then in a special bulletin, news came over that the delegates had voted 98–91 to return to work on Tuesday, almost a year exactly since the Strike began – **THE STRIKE IS OVER**. Arthur Scargill had to go out and personally inform his men it was over, a lot of them were angry, mostly because of the uncertainty over what will

happen to the men who were sacked in the dispute. Arthur says the dispute will continue opposing any closures, because there was no negotiated settlement. Went to gig later at Netherthird with Brian, was a bit apprehensive as it's a militant area, and I would be regarded as a Scab, but nothing was said all night, any miners there seemed subdued, and involved with their own thoughts. It was a good gig though, band went down well. Got home 12pm.

Monday 4 March, 1985
Felt rather tired at work today. It's quite hectic playing in the Group at weekends and working at the pit all week. Heard that the Scottish Executive under Mick McGahey had voted 7–6 to continue the Strike, but nearly all the locals that are still out, including the hard core Netherthird boys, are all starting back tomorrow. The headlines on the national papers were quite subdued really, I suppose everyone realises there are no winners in this Strike. The Kent and Scottish Areas say they'll stay out until they can get an amnesty for the men sacked in the dispute. The Scottish Area Director, Albert Wheeler, says there'll be <u>no</u> amnesty. On the way home from work in the Parks of Hamilton wire meshed bus, at the bus-stop at the top of Netherthird, a small boy, aged about 13, leathered the bus with a half-brick. The driver stopped and ran after him – but he didn't catch him.

Tuesday 5 March 1985
Was busy at work today, changed shaft gate cylinder on Pit Bottom, then built up new type of cage shuttle, thought up by deputy chief engineer Alex Peters. Heard on New that 5 Kent miners had formed a picket line and stopped Arthur Scargill leading the Yorkshire men back to work. The Netherthird boys arrived out on the backshift, wearing badges which read 'I never Scabbed, '84–'85'. I said hello to Harry Parker and got a mumbled reply.

Tuesday 12 March, 1985
There was a pit-head meeting of the NUM. First I've witnessed since the end of the Strike. They were discussing whether to give 50p off our pay to the pickets who were sacked, and whether to end the Overtime Ban. The crowd of 250 men were quite angry and hostile to one another over the issues, but the Union man gave a good speech and got good order from the men. I don't mind paying 50p to the sacked men, and I'm not fussy what happens about the Overtime Ban.

Wednesday 13 March, 1985
Felt really exhausted at work today. Had to go down pit with John Gibson to fit a big gear wheel onto the inset level Pit Bottom creeper. I had to crawl about in 6 inches of mucky water in a space about 3ft square, to try and manoeuvre it into position. It was a fuckin terrible job!!! That's what I really hate about the pit, men having to crawl around in muck like animals. Then the under manager cut our time because we lowsed 5 minutes early, the bastard. Got home and went to bed at 4pm, never got back up, made piece at 1am, went back to bed.

Wednesday 27 March, 1985
Got up 6am. It's very clear daylight now when I get up. The main topic at work today was the guys who work in the washing plant getting their redundancy interviews. Seemingly they've to be transferred to Killoch Pit, with the £1,800 transfer fee. Most of them want to finish up with redundancy though, and the management seems to be refusing them this, even though NCB Chief, Ian MacGregor, said on national news last night that any man would get his redundancy if he so wished. The men were really angry, and started to smash things up in the workshop. Probably hear tomorrow what the outcome will be. The national levy to give the sacked men the 50p levy was defeated (56%–46%). Arthur Scargill had flown to Russia this

week on what was purported to be Union business.

Tuesday 2 April, 1985
Still feeling quite tired. Saw personnel manager, Ian Campbell, today. He says if I could be accepted for a course at Uni or College then I could probably get my redundancy money. I've thought about it for a while, and if I don't begin to do something constructive with my life now then I'll be stuck in a dead end job, ad-infinitum. I think I would be a lot happier doing something I liked doing. The news announced today that 8 Scottish pits are earmarked for closure, they include 4 in Fife and Barony (my pit) and Killoch in Ayrshire. We seemingly have two years to go.

Wednesday 3 April, 1985
All the talk at work today centred round the news that the pit was to close. Everyone was in a 'couldn't care less' mood. I sat about all day, hardly did any work, nobody seemed to be bothering much. The boys from the Washer got their interviews and most of them finished up. Bobby Finlay got £5,000, Mick Stewart got £17,000, and at least 15 others finished up. If I can get something positive arranged regarding further education then I'll try and get out as well.

PART TWO

Come All Ye Bold Miners

The Coal

The black heirt o Scotland aye-an-oan beats,
Laid doun ower sixty million year;
Riches frae the Carboniferous Age.
Dense forests daurk, whaur nae bird e'er did sing,
Whaur nae insect or dragonfly e'er flew,
Amang the endless aeons o seelent trees.
An auncient Eden whaur anely a souch o wuin
Disturbed the quate primordial warld
O lang ago extinct Lepidendrons,
The fern-lyk fronds o strange Pteridosperms,
An stately seas o towerin Calamites;
Twa hunner an fifty million year ago,
The coal wis formed.

Wha first discernt the black-stane hud a uise?
Some auncient tribe, sat hunkert roond their fire,
Wid aiblins set alowe some ootcrop seam,
An grunt – 'Luiks lyk we're oantae somethin here!'
The sairchin human mind wid suin unraivel
Magick alchemy lockt athin the stane,
An thaim wha kent its saicret properties,
O hou tae meld ae metal wi anither,
Wid be revered as shamans, God-lyk men.
They wid be yirdit wi the pomp an splendour
O kings an potentates o future ages;
Laid oot wi aa the graith an gear o power.
Syne tho, aa coin looses its bricht mintage,
Howkin coal becam a mundane thing;
Medieval monks frae Melrose an Newbattle
Wir gien the richt, frae Kings, tae win the coal,
An syne coal-heughs at Dailly an Kirkoswald,
Saw God catch oan – 'Let's exploit the warkers!'

Aeneas Sylvius stuid dumbfoundit when,
He witnessed, staunin ootby some kirk-yett –
'Near naukit beggars, joy upon their faces,
When gien a puckle o black-stanes as alms' –
The Kirk wis ne'er sweir tae turn a shillin.
A hunner year syne Hector Boece wis quoted:
'In Fyffe ar won black stanis
Quilk ha sa intollerable heit
Quhair they are kendillit
That they resolve and meltis irne
And are therefore richt proffitable
For operation of smithis' –
Coal wis here tae stey.

Draconian laws an statutes wir set doun,
Tae keep the miners shacklet tae the darg.
Faithers an sons, boond tae the mine fir life,
Slaves in aa but name – a cless apairt;
In Holyrood's ain 'Habeas Corpus Act',
Aa, but the colliers, wir tae be includit,
An they wir trait lik cattle, waur nor beasts.
They wrocht in Bell-Pits, Stair-Pits, In-Gaun E'es,
Whaur lassies, anely eicht or nine year auld,
Wid haul a load abune a hunnerweicht,
Aiblins mair as twenty times a shift,
The heicht o Sanct Paul's Cathedral's lofty dome –
Aye, thon wis 'sair, sair wark' withooten dout.
It taen fowk o a mair enlichtent age
Tae raise their haund an cry 'eneuch's eneuch!'
An eftir 1840's great Commission
Young weans wis banned frae warkin unnergrund –
Tho this in nae wey cowed the shout fir coal.

As output soars, demand outstrips supply,
Market Forces define an shape the laund,
New Cumnock rose an fell wi sic oangauns;
The place that boomed fir mair's a hunner year,
At Bank, Knockshinnoch, aye, an 'Paddy Waddells'!
Hud its back brucken wi the Miners' Strike,
Condemned tae dee a slaw an lingerin daith.
Thatcher's sheddae fell across the place,
An fowk muived South, whaur they could fuin the wark.
Steel-shuttert nou her schemes gied up the ghaist,
An streets yince thrang wi weans grew husht an quate.
Hauf the hooses aa wir redd awa,
The saund sank tae its lowest in the gless –
But the beatin heirt o coal that dinged thaim doun,
Micht see thaim yet be biggit up agane.

The visionary team at ATH
Breathed life intae coal's local heritage.
Thon windin snake, a green arterial bypass,
The muckle conveyor – twelve kilometres lang,
The greatest o its kind in mainland Europe,
Craigmuckloch, aa the wey tae Crowbandsgate,
Thrums an hums, its pulse beats strang wi life;
An engineering feat tae rival Watt,
Or e'en Newcomen's 'Atmospheric Engine'.
The rich black veins still wrocht fir Scotland's weill,
Rax ower the shooder o Parnassus hill,
Radius curves, sinuous an subliminal,
Ablow the skyline, huggin evri contour,
Past the ruint herds hoose at Craigshiel,
Craigdullyeart's lang abandoned gloomy caverns,
Whaur miners frae anither age aince laboured,
The kilns forleitit whaur they brunt the Lime,
Fir aa the warld lik Reformation ruins,

Whaes cipher bides tho – 1837.
Deid industries ligg, decayin in this laundscape.
Long live the Coal!
The belt drives oan, 500 tonnes an hour.
It disappears ablow a lunky hole,
Then shoots alang the back o Watsonburn.
There's some regrets the wanton despoliation;
This aince wis Wull's cauf-kintra as a boy,
Lang-syne he fisht fir broon troot in the Guelt,
An strode throu bent, an sprett, an meadie-gress,
Tae fuin the nests o Merlins, Whaups, Mosscheepers,
Couriet inby the lea o the Rocky Burn,
Ower the saicent stile, an throu the Primrose Wuid
Tae watch thaim feed the quey at High Garleffan –
He swears he'll ne'er walk that wey agane,
Tae witness aa his bairntid swept awa;
Lost fir aye – a laundscape lik the muin.

It's fine tae eulogise anent the past,
We'd aa prefer the 'Blue remembered hills...'
But 'Real Politik' dictates the wey,
Wha'd tak a cut in public services,
Tae pey the lawin fir Ecology?
Don't kid yersel we'll staun an wring oor haunds,
Whae gies a damn fir Whaups when lichts gang oot?
The kintra's cryin oot fir energy,
Will we staund by while Russkies turn the cock aff?
There's boys needs joabs, an Christmas comin oan,
It's twelve-hour shifts, an Sunday double-time,
Aathing ye hae's dug frae Garleffan mine –
The belt drives oan.
The coal skelps past the back o High Polquheys,
Whaur Alistair Black keeks doun at his watch,
A manager steept in 'the getting of coal'

There's black gowd tae be won – an he wull win it.
Whae's treidin in the fuitsteps o the past,
An kens men must be led, an no be driven,
An haimmers hame the rule o 'Safety First'
Tho men wull no aye dae tho as they're bidden,
An accidents, tho rare, can ayeweys heppen,
A sair yin yon, thae boys at Pennyvenie,
While Kirkconnel Miners' Memorial lists,
Raw upon raw, the names o mining's deid,
Thair's mair wir loast in aa Kirkconnel's pits
Than e'er wis loast bi thaim in twa warld wars –
Five thoosan a year dee in China's mines;
Keep mind, auld frien, thon's the price o coal.
But twelve hour shifts is better than the dole,
An mony a man whaes doun upon his luck,
Wha hus a wife a twa bit weans tae cled,
Wid jimp at the chaunce tae drive a dumper truck.
The belt drives oan – the kintra needs the coal.
It dips past Rottenyard tae Crowbandsgate,
Whaur the traivellin triple-stacker doles it oot,
A longitudinal glistnin black stockpile,
That syne is loadit intae gantin wagons,
Tae feed the e'er hungry power stations;
Eggborough, syne Cockenzie an West Burton,
Ratcliffe, Cottam, Drax an Ironbridge.
The coal train rumbles oan intae the gloamin,
Alang the Nith, an unner Corsencon,
A faint corona haps the daurknin hills,
Infernal lichts illuminate the heivins,
Glenmuckloch lowes lik Zola's 'Le Voreux'
While, twenty-fowr seeven, the belt rins oan.

Abune New Cumnock smeek is slawly driftin,
Frae twa, three chimneys dottit roun the toun.
It dissipates mang frosty, skinklin starns.
No mony hooses nou betray a fire,
Cept, aiblins some auld miner's, nou retired
Wha, o a wunter's nicht, sets up a bleeze,
An ne'er thinks oan the heat gien aff his coal,
That eases jynts worn sair wi constant wark,
Wis pitten there in ages lang-syne past,
An whit he's feelin's waarmth hained frae the sun –
Twa hunner an fifty million year ago.

Avisyard Hill

Hauf this giant hillside torn awa,
Bi the merciless maws o giant machines.
Prowlin, prehistoric predators,
Boldly emblazoned 'CAT' or 'JCB',
Backbrekkin toil, the darg o generations,
Redd-up lik sweepins o a baur-room flair,
Till nou we read the story in yer banes;
Stratified layers, the leaves in some auld buik,
Titanic faults and languid folds exposed,
That rax ayont Agricola's dour legions,
Intil a past that's daurk an maist unkent,
When this place wis a forest or a sea.
Your evolution's wrocht nou by new forces,
Wha've biggit here a strange an fremmit Eden;
A man-made loch, hemm't in bi man-made cliffs,
That time wull syne enow claim fir her ain.
Fierce Peregrines wull stoop oan prey frae here,
Wi ne'er a care that this hus no aye bin.

Dalmellington Baun

This room, lik a works canteen; stark, functional,
brichtly lit, austere, fit fir ae purpose –
tae fix these players minds anely oan music.
Nae clock hings oan the wa, there's nae distraction,
juist the muckle banners; 'Scottish Champions',
clear mindin o their pridefou pedigree.
The piece they're warkin oan's bi Gilbert Vinter,
bound fir the Nationals, comin up in Mairch,
(a wit declares 'a swatch o *Arban's Tutor*!).
'Salute to Youth' is technically demandin,
fierce chromatic rins o semi-quavers,
pushin principle players tae their leemits;
concentration etcht upon their faces.
While Airchie, their baun-maister, teases oot
abeelities they thocht they nevir hud;
'A braw wee trio – when ye hear the pairts!'
'Gin thon judge hus goat lugs – best bet, he's listenin!'
an repetition o some fykie pairt
draws frae thaim honed an purposefou perfection.
Ae meenit, saftly, pianissimo,
Syne, stabbin fiercely his conductor's wand,
A snarlin Sforzando, thunderous in its micht!
Oan Airchie's score, 'Eroico' unnerlined,
'Heroically'! juist listen, an ye'll hear,
that smeddum wrocht frae ither generations.
Likesay, the bluid o heroes' in their veins;
whaes faither's faithers wrocht at Pennyvenie,
in Minnivey, at Burnton, an the Beoch,
the huddlet group in thon auld photiegraph,
wi miners cap-laumps, playin Christmas carols,
a history that's leevin, breathin yet.
The Silver Baun, a muckle great machine,

whaes pairts must wark in harmony thegaither,
lik some vast Winding Engine, cast frae bress,
raisin tae the licht its praicious cargo.

Keir Hardie (1856–1915)

Born intae puirtith, weel ye kent the darg,
Rinnin messages at anely seeven year auld.
Doun the pit at ten, trappin air fir miners,
Drivin pownies, hewin the three fuit seam,
Calloused hauns, sair uised tae pick an shovel.
'Lad o Pairts', ye lairnt tae read an write,
Bi caunle licht, aback a ten hour shift.
Yer vyce rung oot – the cry wis 'naitrel justice!'
The cry the bosses ne'er liked tae hear –
'Agitator!' 'Rabble-Rouser!' 'Trouble-Maker!'
An syne the wird goat roond – yer nem blacklistit.
Yer answer tae thaim aa? Defend the richt!
Clingin fast tae the anchor o yer faith,
Ye focht fir aa the fowk tae yer latest braith;
First Labour MP, anti-Monarchist,
Wha stuid wi Pankhurst an her suffragettes,
Else, back agin the wa, at pit or mill.
Socialist, Humanist, Pacifist,
Yer souch o raison tint i' the wuin,
O the war they ettled wid end aa wars,
A dove o peace amang a pack o wolves –
It aiblins bruck yer heirt at the hinnerend.
Here, at the Baird, yer legacy remains;
The laump that aince ye held athin yer haund,
That shone, in each coalface, still raxin oot,
Growne weaker, aye, but still-an-oan, it lowes.

Lowsed

Greenhill and Farden Avenue, aamaist gane,
'All items of value have been removed'.
Forleitit shrubs, the rose an honeysuckle,
The vanisht fowk, wha warkt an leeved an luved.
Wa's daubed bi feral weans whaes names remain;
Gary, Bob an Dib, Dylan, Lee an Wullie,
Ubiquitous graffiti, rude an phallic,
That boasts o 'NC boys on top – non-stop'
 Whaes shattert hames abide lik the condemned,
The yella executionered JCB.
Whiles faur awa ayont thon distant rig,
Ahint the remnants o the 'Stage-Coach' wuid,
The green shuits o prosperity appear;
Whaur men howk coal that's sair'd New Cumnock weel,
Thon gey sair darg they've tholed twa hunner year.
Their pastimes still the same; the 'Dugs' an 'Doo's'.
Ye'll see thaim oot the Mansfield walkin grews,
Whiles here the doocots staun that's still their pride,
That hauds their howps, their wee bit shot at glory.
These squeakers here, thae Pied an Blue Bar cocks,
Micht see their names enshrined in local lore,
An emulate 'Shot Wattle's' win at Rennes.
Fir aince these men wir caged lik beasts theirsel,
An flew in shafts o intake airway air.
At least nou they've a freedom o a sorts,
An like their Doo's their thochts can aiblins soar,
Speerits lowsed tae dream o whit micht be.

'Shot Wattle' was a very famous racing pigeon. It won the premiere event
in this sport, the race from Rennes, in France, in 1912.

Memorials

Aa alang the length o the Afton Glen,
Lie reuch wee cundies built o wuid an stane.
The yin ah'm sittin in's cried 'Windmill View'
An, like it says, ayont it oan the hill,
There's thirteen giant turbines can be seen.
Nae dout ava that miners built these howffs,
Stane oan tap o stane, they've bigged thaim up,
Their lang redundant haunds keep mind the skills
O hou tae build a pack tae haud a ruif.
Tricks o the tred haun't doun frae faithers' faithers,
In facelines o the Barony or Killoch;
Minedrivers wha spent decades at the brushin,
Creatin roadways faur ablow the grunnd,
Whaes airches nou nae dout time wull hae bucklet,
As time wull shairly sair tae wear us aa.
Thae auld men wha sit here an courie in,
An shelter in these queer bields frae the blast,
Wull reminisce aboot a warld that's gane,
Hunkert oan a baton fir a sate,
They'll craic anent auld friens, wha's deid, or deein;
While oan the hill the Wind Fairm's monstrous blades
Are haunds o clocks, that tick awa the years.

Disaster

The seeventh o September, nineteen fifty,
The legend etcht oan these worn mairble heidstanes;
'Knockshinnoch, Knockshinnoch, Knockshinnoch...'
Whan the warld's een briefly lichtit oan New Cumnock,
A hunner an twenty nine men wir entombed,
When thon inrush o glaur swept throu the pit.
The heroic rescue attempt that follaed;
That saved aamaist thaim aa – but these thirteen.
Stories haundit doun o local courage,
Men wha wrocht lik stirks tae save their friens;
Brent new ropes wi ten-ton brekkin strains
Wir snapt lik threid bi heavin desprait haunds.
Fowk drove theirsels ayont aa human leemits.
The photies in the archives at the 'Baird'
Show seelent waitin croods wi fearfu faces;
Faithers, mithers, dochters, wives an sons.
Their shawls an bunnets o anither age,
That kent gey weel the price fir whit coal's won,
Wha gied thenks fir the men whae aa goat rescued,
But widnae lea the ithers in that place,
They won their menfolk back, aye evri wan.
Sae nou these comrades ligg here aathegaither,
In this safe bield amang the braes o hame;
Sleep soun, the darg is ower, ye've earnt yer rest.

Triptych: 'Maggie... Maggie... Maggie...'

i) The Lanely Daith o Maggie Thatcher

The day they're mindin her wi hauf-mast flags,
Neist week they'll spend ten million oan her kistin,
Whiles Tony Blair, wi grief his een are mistin,
Nae dout he'll bray wi aa the ither windbags,
Wha'll gaither in the House tae sing her praise;
They'll deftly whitewaash ower Pinochet,
Mandela's refusal tae jine her fir some tea...
But frien ah've mind o ither lang-gane days,
New Cumnock here in Ayrshire aince wis bien,
Wi pits an factories pourin wages in,
Nou evriwhaur ye luik the place is duin,
Her 'legacy' tae us? a thing obscene!
Her room's redd-up an trig nou at the Ritz –
Mercat forces wull see she isnae missed.

ii) *Maggie's Funeral*

Tae the tune o 'Mairi's Wedding'

Chorus
Step we gaily oan we go
Heel fir heel and toe fir toe
Airm in airm and row and row
Aa fir Maggie's funeral

Turned the news oan jist the day,
Maggie Thatcher's passed away,
Hip-Hooray the miners say,
We're weel shoat o Maggie!

Tebbit, Rifkind, Tony Blair,
Heseltine wi gowden hair,
Tellin us that she wis rerr,
Wha're ye kiddin!? Maggie!?

In the Falklands they're aa sick,
They'll be sell't aff double-quick,
Fir tae pey aff Cameron's tick,
They'll aa miss their Maggie.

Here in Ayrshire we goat screwed,
Aa oor miners oan the Buroo,
Noo a 'bedroom tax', whit's new?
You sure fucked us Maggie!

Nae mair pits fir her tae close,
Nou that daith's gien her a dose,
As she passes haud yer nose,
There goes stinkin Maggie.

Nou that Maggie's doun in hell,
The furnaces they'll hae tae sell,
'We're privatised!' the Deevils yell,
'Why did we tak Maggie!?'

iii) Everything Must Go...

The Kaiser Biscuit American Bald Eagle
Realised almost half a million dollars;
More absurd and obscene lots soon followed;
A set of ten gilt miniature oil barrels...
Mencken's *Dictionary of Quotations*,
Hammered down for only fourteen grand;
An Emes and Barnard George IV inkstand;
Cinderella flounce and ostentation.
But now the room's abuzz, they look askance,
Blood drips from each hedgefund manager's maw,
As ravenously they surge and push and paw,
For surely now, the pièce de résistance;
Kellingley Colliery and its miners renowned,
Who'll start the bidding! Surely, come, a pound...?

On Tuesday 15 December, 2015, Christie's Auction House held a sale of
property that had belonged to the late British Prime Minister, Margaret
Thatcher. The sale realised more than £4.5 million pounds. *The Guardian*
dryly stated that 'she was worth more dead than alive'. Thatcher presided
over one of the most bitter industrial disputes of the 20th century; the
1984–85 Miners' Strike. Two days after this sale the last deep coal mine
in Britain, Kellingley Colliery in North Yorkshire, closed.

PART THREE

Colliery Crambo Clink

Note on 'Frozen'

'Frozen' deals wi the horrors o workin oan the pit-heid during wintertime. Summertime oan the pit-heid wis indeed a pleasant affair, but winters wir a cauld, depressin, endless nightmare! Robert Service (a man wha hus buits ah cuidnae begin tae lace) is wan o Scotlands greatest poets. If you have not read his work then ye should pop doon tae yer library an remedy this oversight as soon as possible. Ah mak nae apologies fir plagiarising a line or three fae him in this poem, ah think he wid agree wi the sentiments in it.

Ian Nairn (Big Nairny) is a legendary driver o buses in East Ayrshire. He drove fir the auld SMT bus company fir years, afore they were aa taen owre bi 'Soapy' Soutar an his crew. Buses cuid, an did, become stranded in the icy, untreated roads o the hoosing schemes o mining villages. On the occasion mentioned here the miners wir obviously reticent tae disembark fae the bus an gie it a push oot o the drift theirsels (turkeys votin fir Christmas!) A wag at the back o the bus did indeed shout fir thaim tae phone Jock Stirling (the colliery personnel manager) tae personally come an shove the bus. This did not transpire!

'Pish Hoose Spickets!' – this wonderfully descriptive phrase refers tae the auld fashioned 'ootside conveniences' o the auld 'miners rows' cottages, wi their auld brass watter taps. They wir aamaist invariably swathed in reams o lagging in winter tae prevent them fae freezin.

The 'Power-Pack'; this wis a large electrically powered hydraulic pump that wis used aa owre the pit in many different applications, e.g. Raising/Lowering Face line supports at the coal-face, operating hydraulic rams tae open chutes an hoppers, etc...) Oan the Surface they could be prone tae freezing in winter, especially if switched aff fir ony length o time (static liquid bein mair apt tae freeze).

'Gleamin White Helmets an Muslin Scarves!' – managers,

chiefs an gaffers ayeways appeared oan the pit-heid wi shiny new helmets an brilliant white scarves (this wis a great help tae 'Five-Eichters', as ye cuid spot thaim a mile awa!). The scarves wir made oot o lengths o 'cheese' or muslin cloth which cam fae the stores. Ah never ever kent o onybody bein able tae get their hauns oan this mystical material, ordinary mortals could nevir hope tae obtain or aspire tae wearin a white Muslin scarve!

No.3 and No.4 shafts – pits aye hud at least twae shafts. The 'Intake' (or Ingress) shaft, which drew in fresh air, an the 'Return' (or Egress) shaft, which hud huge extractor fans tae draw the stale spent air oot o the pit. Obviously the fresh air bein drawn in wis a lot caulder than the spent air, which hud traivellt throu the pit an wis therefore quite warm when it wis expelled. The 'return' shaft, in this case No.4 shaft at the Barony, wis situated in a slightly lower geographical position than the 'Intake' shaft, an wis perhaps a hauf a mile or sae fae the 'Intake' shaft, tae aid the flow o the air. In winter, because air wis drawn doon the 'Intake' shaft and watter constantly ran doon it as weel, then in really severe spells o cauld weather large chunks o ice could form in the shaft. This could be a very dangerous situation if large pieces o ice broke aff an fell doon the shaft. Oan these occasions men wid no be allowed tae traivel in the shaft and wid therefore hae tae ascend the 'Return' shaft (whaur there wis nae ice), a trip which meant a lengthy walk in usually bitter, inclement conditions, a cause fir great greetin an girnin agane amangst the five-eichters! Monies the time ah witnessed the 'Shaftsmen' descend the pit cages, attached wi safety harnesses, an lean oot owre a drap o a thoosan feet or mair an chip awa at this ice wi pick-axes tae try an brek it aa aff, a stinkin, freezing, horrible an dangerous joab!

Frozen

I

Miners, thae troglodyte heroes, wha trauchle unner the grund,
Moan when summer's nigh, an they descend fae the 'Heat o the Sun',

They curse the cushy surface boys, in wuidyaird or sawmill,
And pine fir lazy summer days spent lazin oan the 'Hill',

Whaur gentle zephyrs waft, and ye hear the gentle bleat,
O lambs wha seek the shade, tae avoid the searin heat,

Boys strip aff tae vest an shorts, an gie their feet a treat,
Dippin thaim in the 'Reservoir Pond', as they enjoy their piece,

Tae say that they sunbathed aa day isnae quite the truth,
They gien the 'Board' three hours at least, afore lyin oan the roof!

Aye, summer's grand fir surface boys, but salad days syne go,
Cam the Autumnal equinox, the Sun sinks red and low,

Leaves softly faa, a carpet spun o yella, green and gold,
November's gale sends tumblin craws wheelin to and fro,

Fearfully, eyes peer, oot o evri surface hovel,
An wi each miraculous snowflake, they anxiously eye the shovels!

Robert Service, whose 'Law of the Yukon', spelt it oot quite plain,
'Send not your foolish and feeble, send me your strong and your sane!'

The Yukon got the strong an sane, but in some playful irony,
The foolish an the feeble, wir aa sent tae the 'Barony'!

Thus, Friday, Third o February, in nineteen eichty three,
The Car-Hall fitters sat in their howff, wi scaldin mugs o tea,

Ootside the blizzard howled an blew, richt aff the Beaufort Scale,
A chill drave throu yer long-johns, that pierced lik a driven nail!

Frae his pocket Harry Parker drew, his faithful auld chronometer,
Then tapped his pipe oan the side, o his treasured oak barometer,

Nae suiner hud he tapped, when it fell, wi an awfy crashin soond!
An a chillin portent fillt the howff, wi a sense o impendin doom!

Hughie Richie tried tae laugh it aff, 'Ach, dinnae look sae glum!
We kent the Mercury hud sunk gey low, – noo its hit the grund!'

Wee Harrys meteorological joy, lay sadly waither-beaten,
An gaitherin a handfu o cogs an springs, he luikt gey near tae greetin,

Misty eyed, he eulogised, owr the stricken heirloom,
Wee Hughie Allan (a pragmatist!), went oot tae fetch the broom!

In a daurk recess its dial lay, the needle jammed at 'FREEZE',
As tho the fates hud aa conspired, tae bring us tae wir knees!

The veesionary powers o Coleridge, couldnae chronicle Harry's loss,
His barometer cam tae symbolise, the mythical albatross!

An fae the 'Ancient Mariners' icy polar tomb,
An Arctic wind cam rushin, tae confirm Wee Harry's gloom,

II

The weekend passed, the weathermen gasped, it hud never luikt sae
    ominous,
As an Arctic front encroached the laund, and suin it wis upon us!

Thirty miners sat oan a bus, its rear wheels spun in a drift,
An tho Big Nairny curst an swore, he couldnae mak it shift,

'Richt boys! Oot an gie's a shove! We'll suin hae the Horrals birlin!'
A wag replied, 'A shove? ye better send fir Big Jock Stirling!!'

An hour later the Barony emerged, fae the frozen mist,
Like Sleeping Beauty risin, when frae her slumbers kissed,

Transformed, by aa the ice intae some hellish Santa's grotto,
Bleary miners disembarked, maist o thaim still half blotto!

Ye widnae believe hou cauld it wis, frae John O' Groats tae Dover,
An the Car-Hall confirmed ma worst nichtmare; Hell hud frozen over!

Each Ram and Flap, Valve and Stop, Hose, Steam-Trap and Shunky
Lay there, petrified, like some taxidermist's monkey!

Transfixed, lik frogs in a heidlamp, we tuik in the awfy scene,
An vainly pu'ed aa the haundles, convinced it wis a dream,

Vainly we tried then realised, that we stuid oan the abyss,
Napoleon's retreat fae Moscow? a picnic compared tae this!

Like wounded Lions we crept tae the howff, oor metaphorical thicket,
Then lingert till the heatin gien oot, wrapt up like pish-hoose spickets!

The Five-Eichters 'Baa-ed!' and 'Maa-ed!' as they thronged up evri
   gantry,
They stuid there in dumb expectancy, lik dugs ootside a pantry,

Quickly re-groupin we counter-attacked, wi haundfus o oily waste,
An sent fir Acetylene Torches, which suin arrived post-haste,

Banks o valves wir doused, in ony liquid deemed tae be flammable,
Wee Harry tossed a match (crossed his Rubicon, jist lik Hannibal),

The valves slaistert in evrithing, fae WD40, tae Pernod!
Erupted in flames, jist lik a scene, straicht oot o Dantes Inferno!

Miners descendit tae their comfy lairs, waarm pipes an cosy cundys,
While we stuid frozen, chilled tae the bane, an *this* wis only Monday!

III

They call it stormy Monday, but Tuesday's twice as bad!
We felt lik dementit Russians, pinned doun at Stalingrad!

The Mercury plummeted aff the scale, haltin at *minus fourteen!*
Michael Fish said, frae his cosy neuk, 'It's the worst ah've ever seen!'

'Ye don't say, Michael!?' as we huddled roond the wee electric fire,
Wee Hughie said 'At Colditz, ye cuid at least jump oan the wire!'

Hughie Richie, tae his great dismay, received an awfy shock,
When ordered tae 'Get yokit'!' afore the knock struck eicht o'clock!

We wandered roond wi haund-lamps, tryin tae thaw the frozen system,
As wan valve opened, the next yin froze, the cauld it grew mair
   fearsome!

Wednesday the 'PowerPack' gied oot, 'Big Joab' wis sent tae fix it,
Piece-time arrived, Big Hughie retired, tae hae hissel a tit-bit,

Noo it disnae tak Newton or Einstein, tae reach the next conclusion,
Or an expert in pairticle physics, or even nuclear fusion,

Flowin watter is less apt tae freeze (that's whit ah lairnt at college),
Switch aff a 'Pack'? *at minus fourteen?* shows a glarin lack o
   knowledge,

The Dirt-Hopper Ram, an evri hose, froze stiff an stark as daith,
Fir the sake o a Kit-Kat, Big Hughie hud robbed the Barony o its braith!

Gleamin white helmets an white muslin scarves, suin swarmt
   evriwhere,
The 'Spanish Inquisition', suin hud Hughie tearin his hair!

Thursday – Big Hughie aff seeck – an the Pit in a grip o iron,
Shrouded in mist, the Horrals kept their precious cargo flyin!

Wee Hughie Allan (thocht he wis fly!), descended tae the Bottom,
But Fate intervened, Wee Hughie lairnt the folly o his wisdom,

Jist lik a moose in the cosy howff, Wee Hugh felt nary a draft!
Unaware, that faur abune his heid, frost wis icin up the Shaft!

'Nae men tae ascend Number Three!' the Intake shaft wis closed,
Abune, a White-Out Hell hud raged as wee Hugh gently dozed,

'Ye'll hae tae use the Return Shaft, Hugh', a trek tae Number Fowr,
Then a twa mile hike throu the blizzard, the thocht made Wee
   Hugh cower!

Staggerin blin throu the snawdrifts, stumblin half-mad, throu the gale!
Featureless! Frozen! Forsaken! he wis cairtit in, stiff as a nail!

Friday – Wee Hughie aff seeck! – an the outluik still appeared bleak!
Men were pheesically seeck! – an we prayed fir the end o the week!

'The coldest spell oan record!' oor Michael smirkt fae the telly,
Wi bated braith the long-range forecast turnt wir knees tae jelly!

But science, as weel as nature, sometimes fails tae gang tae plan,
An as usual, Michael Fish an his team goat the hale thing wrang,

Wee Harry an me, the last tae survive the rigours o the cauld,
Wi the pallor o ghaists cam staggerin past, the Barony's main
    Time-Hall,

We emerged frae the baths, an shared a glance, mingled wi grief an pain,
An as we waitit oan wir buses, *it slowly, began, tae rain!*

Note on 'The Wreck o the Auld Number Nine'

There wis an auld green loco at the Barony Pit, though its real number wis Number Seventeen. Poetic licence dictates tho that number nine is a much mair suitable word tae use fir rhymin purposes! Roond aboot nineteen eichty three there wis some kind o industrial crisis (it micht huv bin tae dae wi the Dockers or fuel), onywey, it led tae a worry that fuel supplies micht become scarce. Therefore they did renovate and restore this auld steam loco in the event that they widnae be able tae obtain fuel fir the Diesel Locomotives. These auld 'Pugs' wir uised tae shunt wagons o coal and supplies roond the pit-heid. Ah even goat tae drive it yince, ah pu'd the big lever that opened the steam valve an moved it aboot twenty feet doon the track! Thus ah'll be yin o the few in ma generation that can honestly claim tae hae driven a steam train!

'Sports Division' wis a company founded bi New Cumnock entrepreneur an 'Lad o Pairts' Sir Tam Hunter. This wis a hugely successful business supplyin sports goods in the high street (an occasionally in lay-bys!). Tam is o course noo the richest man in the Universe, and seems quite happy aboot this. His family hud fir generations, been grocers in New Cumnock.

'Dunsinane' is Macbeth's castle in that eponymous Shakespearian tragedy. It's a name that romantically inclined types in Scotland hae hijacked fir their new wee bungalows.

The Mauchline Basin Plain is the geographical term fir the huge coal field that exists beneath Ayrshire. It contains the largest reserves o coal in the United Kingdom.

Adam Gall and Alex Jess wir twae respected senior tradesmen at the Barony. They were excellent journeyman engineers wha did their best tae impart their hard-won knowledge oan tae me – this sadly wis a task tho that wis beyond even their undoubted abilities!

The 'Reservoir Pond'; maist pits hud a large Resorvoir/Pond, which was the source o aa the vast amounts o watter that wir required underground, i.e. fir hydraulic systems, fire-fighting, dust suppression, etc.

Wull Timpany worked as the baths attendant and also as a first-aider and medical attendant at the Medical Centre, folk lik Wull wir usually described by fellow miners as 'A B— wi a guid joab!'.

The *Miners' Weekly* (some poetic licence... the paper wis the *Scottish Miner*); A weekly newspaper dealing exclusively wi miners, their lives and issues, e.g. Pay-rises (Ayeways popular!), Maggie Thatcher, an her pairtner in crime Ian MacGregor (ayeways unpopular!), gairdenin, Dugs an Doos, Sports (Fitba, Boolin...), Gala days etc. Ah still hae a few copies o it preserved fir posterity.

The Wreck o the Auld Number Nine

When we were young we aa hud dreams,
Like captaining famous fitba teams,

Or flyin rockets tae the Moon,
An diggin up hoards o gold doubloons,

Makkin a Billion, lik 'Sports Division',
By sellin gutties oan television,

Or becoming a name in high finance,
An leadin the boardroom a merry dance,

Makin yer name as a great Exchequer,
By knockin tuppence aff a litre,

But dreams? they're only meant fir weans,
As we grow up their magic wanes,

Their golden lustre turns tae tin,
The futile hopes o a Lottery win,

A new car, or a trip tae Spain,
Or a bungalow, caa'd 'Dunsinane',

Oor adult dreams seem as mundane,
As, ----- being the driver o a train!

But wait a meenit, drivin a train,
Wis wance the dream o every wean,

An tae this vision one man hud clung,
Namely oor Hero, Alex Young.

Noo Alex wis banksman at the pit,
An if in his howf ye chanced tae sit,

Alex wid regale ye wi his tales,
O days spent by the iron rails,

Fir jist a keek at the 'Flyin Scotsman',
Oan its record breakin run tae Euston,

In some reverie, like a waking dream,
Alex re-lived the great days o steam,

He knew the number o every train,
That e'er crossed the Mauchline Basin Plain,

The mention o modern locomotion,
Wis apt tae cause a great commotion,

'Diesels!' Alex wid splutter wi rage,
Rammin a mine-caur ontae the cage,

'Nothin but an abomination!
Gie me guid auld steam navigation!'

Unbeknownst though tae Alex Young,
The Sword o Fate wis being hung,

As he slipped tae the canteen fir a snack,
A sicht halted Alex in his tracks!

He yelled as he spilt his scaldin Coco,
Fir there in the yaird stood a big green Loco!

His pulse wis racin, his chest grew ticht,
Alex hud fallen in love at first sicht!

COLLIER LADDIE

But whaur hud she come fae? the 'Auld Number Nine'?,
An why wis she there?, at the Barony Mine?,

The answer tae this puzzlin enigma,
Wis the Arabs latest oil embargo,

Prince Ali'd loast his shirt, doon at the Casino,
Noo the mugs owre here hud tae pay fir his beano!

The 'Wheels o Industry' still hud tae turn,
Although there wis nae Diesel left tae burn,

Diesel, so tae speak, wis oan the dole,
So hail! the return o 'Old King Coal'!

Alex gloated as the Diesels lay forlorn,
Steams golden age hud been re-born!

Though in need o some minor renovation,
The fitters commenced a full restoration,

Adam Gall wis sent tae sort oot the mess,
Ably assisted, by one Alex Jess,

Unawares, they were spied oan at every turn,
By the banksman whose youthful ambition did burn,

Though fate hud robbed him o his aspiration,
His mind wis noo fixed oan a suicide mission,

Obsession hud clouded his feverish brain,
By hook or by crook! HE WID DRIVE THAT TRAIN!

Adam Gall, meanwhile, wis hivvin some fun,
Takin 'Auld Number Nine' oan her maiden run,

Roond the Pit-heid, past the reservoir pond,
Doon past the baths, the Sawmill and beyond,

She proved quite an inspirational sicht,
As she huffed an puffed, wi aa her micht,

An soon every day her route she wis plyin,
Wi a rake o hutches, doon tae a wee sidin,

That nestled alongside the big main line,
Thence oan tae ships anchored oan the Tyne,

Thus 'Auld Number Nine' plied her merry way,
Up an doon wi her hutches every day,

Her driver though, wis a complete unknown,
A wee wizened welshman, caa'd Ivor Jones,

Noo he liked his drink, an wis a bit o a skiver,
The men christened him — 'Ivor the Engine-Driver'!

Alex though, knew whit wis whit, fu brawlie,
An Ivor an him soon grew richt pally,

He plied him wi drink, he plied him wi cigs,
Invited him roond fir a dram at his digs,

Soon Alex wis rewarded fir aa his pains,
An at piece-time he slyly boarded the train,

As Ivor explained the gleamin controls,
Alex made his big play, – fir Ivor's soul!

Fae his pooch he brocht oot a bottle o 'Bells!
'It's yours! if ah can drive her back massel!'

Ivor's mind wis torn, this could be risky,
He thocht fir twa seconds, then grabbed the whisky!

'Auld Number Nine' pu'ed awa at full throttle,
Ivor, in delight, screwed the tap aff the bottle,

Thus, a 'Crash-Course' began,in steam navigation,
As Alex keenly listened tae Ivor's oration,

Ivor's droning lecture grew more protracted,
Wha could blame Alex fir being distracted,

He thocht o the crowds, doon at Euston Station,
And envisaged the scenes, the standin ovation,

As in his minds eye, the 'Blue Riband' he won,
As he taen the 'Scotsman's' record, at owre the ton!

Oh, Alex! ye should've been payin attention!
Noo the dials ye scan wi incomprehension!

The bafflin array o haundles an levers,
Hiv marked ye doon as an under-achiever!

At the siding, Ivor dismounted, hauf-buckled,
An, staggerin forrit, the hutches uncoupled,

The bottle o whisky, noo drained tae the dregs,
He mounted the platform, noo oan his last legs,

The return journey noo, a daudle! a stroll!
Ivor haun't owre 'Auld Number Nine's controls,

He'd tocht Alex weel, he could dae nae mair,
An cradlin the bottle, he sank tae the flair!

Alex wis lost noo in his childhood dream,
Throttle wide open, wi a fu heid o steam,

His joy wis boundless fir all tae see,
An he tooted the whistle in childish glee!

Roond the bend 'Number Nine' cam puffin,
Ivor's een, in deep sleep, were shuttin,

Doon the track 'Number Nine' cam roarin!
Wee Ivor, in a heap, lay snorin,

Then Alex grin began tae waver,
Whilst Ivor, in the DTS, havered,

Whilst being coached, though he hudnae shone,
He'd grasped the theory o gettin her gaun,

But as, owre the rails, the auld loco stoatit,
A thocht occurred, – 'HOW THE HELL DID YE STOP IT!'

Panic ensued, an he kicked wee Ivor,
But he couldnae rouse the senseless driver,

Past the washer 'Number Nine' cam rushin,
Then she howled richt owre the level-crossin,

Her whistle shrieked in over-drive,
Pit-heid workers jumped fir their lives,

Puir Alex shut baith his een in terror,
The Pit-heid buffers loomin nearer,

Richt through the buffers wi a michty 'Crash!'
The 'Auld Number Nine' landed wi a 'Splash!'

The 'Deid-Man's Haundle' leapt fae Alex haun,
As she cam tae licht in the Reservoir Pond!

Before she sank he grabbed wee Ivor,
An swam tae shore wi the lone survivor,

Oor fascination fir horror never ceases,
Even Alex M'Ginn abandoned his pieces!

The crowd aa cheered, an craned their necks,
As Alex dragged Ivor fae the wreck,

As he slunk through the crowds, tae resume his station,
Wull Timpany commenced the resuscitation.

POST-SCRIPT

Post-traumatic Stress is a curious thing,
Puir Ivor, he couldnae remember a thing,

Alex Young accepted the accolades meekly,
Even his photo in the *Miners' Weekly*!

That showed the hero o the Barony Mine,
Beside the wreck o the 'Auld Number Nine!'

Who's happily ensconced in his 'Banks'! once again,
An, strange though it seems, never talks aboot trains,

Wishes an dreams? In yer mind leave them planted,
Cause, if ye're unlucky, wan day they'll be granted!

Note on 'Jim Marr's Disaster'

The maist unbelievable thing aboot aa these poems is that a wheen o the incidents mentioned are aa, wi few exceptions, maistly true. If ye get a chance hae a read at Guthrie Hutton's excellent book *Mining: Ayrshires Lost Industry* and oan page seeventy six ye'll see the actual bog that Jim Marr blew up! (It's the doorway oan the wee buildin oan the left haun side o the main pictur). This book is aamaist indispensable when readin these crambo-clink poems as it shows the pit-heid at the time they wir written and illustrates a great mony o the scenes that are mentioned. Ah went tae the schule wi Jim Marr, he wis aye a likeable character, yin o they folk whaes company ye jist like tae be in, an he's still a likeable character yet. Ah've aaready telt ye that Jim blew up the bog wi Coalzalene, an there wis a 'Stewards Inquiry' intae it.

The poem wis written in the year that New Cumnock's fitba team, the Glenafton Athletic (though in these last few seasons mair lik Pathetic!) hud gotten beat bi Largs Thistle (Free 99s at Nardini's that nicht!) in the semi-final o the Scottish Junior Cup, hence the reference.

'Finals' is self explanatory. Coal Board apprentices goat five attempts at their final exams, an only the brichtest an best passed at the first attempt.

Cable-ends (especially the huge 'Elephant-Trunk' cable ends) wir a 'Bastart o a joab!' that the electricians aa hated wi a vengeance. Imagine wiring a plug wi aboot three hunder wires in it an ye'll hae some idea whit it wis like. The cable wis enclosed in thick, black Bitumen (a sticky tar-like substance), an it wis a helluva joab tae get it aff. Thus the tradesmen aa used Coalzalene tae melt/dissolve it aff (though they werenae meant tae, but they maistly aa did it), which wis a common shortcut fir the joab at that time. Health an Safety types readin this nou wull aa be faintin aboot this!

The Area Training Centre wis at the Barony Pit an Sam Mason wis yin o the heid electrical instructors there. They were ultra-safety conscious at the Training Centre an when ye wir there ye hud tae dae it aa bi the book,

Tho when ye went tae wark at the pit-heid workshoaps the book wis usually flung oot o the windae.

'Moles an Craws': Fairmers in Scotland hae a tradition o hingin deid moles an craws, that they've either shot or trapped, fae fences bi the roadside. There they hing lik latter day victims oan medieval gibbets. Ah don't ken why the fairmers dae this as it disnae seem tae act as ony deterrent tae the moles an craws, wha cairry oan in their recidivist manner thievin an stealin withoot a care.

'Far-Off Run': this wis pit terminology fir a coalface that wis a lang wey fae the Pit Bottom. It wis aye a cause fir moanin an girnin fae tradesman when they wir allocated tae the furthest 'Runs', this meant, o course, that ye bud tae trek a loat further an cairry yer graith a lot longer than wis usual an wis thus a richt scunner!

'Hill-Turn': the 'Hill' wis pit terminology fir workin oan the Surface. The tradesmen hud a work rota that meant that evri sae often ye goat yer twa week stint oan the 'Hill'. The work wis cleaner, usually easier, food wis better (cause ye hud access tae the canteen), an maist tradesmen preferred it. Though there wis aye twa or three greedy buggers that moaned because they loast their enhanced undergrund rates!

Barrheid (Barrhead, in Glasgow) wis the centre for that world renowned 'Shunky' producer and purveyor of bespoke wcs (check them oot fir yersel at Kenny Blackwood's Carrick Quality Bathroom Showrooms in Ayr ('wan tae suit evri arse!') – the famed and legendary Armitage Shanks Company.

Jim Marr's Disaster

Ye've heard o great disasters, ah'm sure ye can bring tae mind,
A dozen or mair great tragedies that've shocked an numbed mankind,

The great *Titanic*, the *Hindenberg*, the Wall Street Crash, the Alamo,
Custer's Last Stand, Hiroshima, an brave Scott's trek tae the Pole!

Potato famines, rice famines, forest fires, earthquakes storms an floods,
Plagues o locusts, plagues o rats, an fatal slides o mud.

They're etched oan oor minds, even etched oan stane, like a biblical
    epistle,
Some, too painful tae contemplate, daur ah mention it?, Largs Thistle!

Sae disaster lurks aa aroond us, just waitin its chance tae strike,
Some think they can even predict it (Nostradamus or David Icke),

Thus throughoot history men hae wept as the Bells of Doom did toll,
But the disaster that befell Jim Marr wis more painful, on the HOLE!

Noo Jim wis a harum-scarum lad, wha liked a laugh an a jovial crack,
He backed the horses, smoked an drank, in buyin his roond he
    wisnae slack!

He passed his finals first attempt, makin the great transition,
O completin his apprenticeship, tae become an electrician,

Jim taen his duties seriously, settin oot wi a manfu will,
Till wan day, due tae an urgent joab, he wis posted tae the Hill,

Jim savoured the lingerin cup o tea, afore they aa goat yokit,
Then Davie Bowie, the chargehaun, cleared his throat an spokit,

Each man wis gien his allotted tasks, Big Davie explained the score,
Jim's face aghast tae learn his fate, a job all sparkies deplore,

'Noo Jim, as sune as ye've redd that binch, an sune as ye are able,
There's fowr big cable ends tae mak up, mark them A.28 Stable!'

Jim's heart fair sank, 'Fowr cable ends! yin wis bad enough!'
But he vowed tae show auld Bowie, he wis made o sterner stuff!

Sae Jim did his best an stuck tae the joab, as weel as he wis able,
But progress wis slow, as some o ye know, cleanin aff the cable,

The Bitumen fairly stuck like glue, gettin even a fraction aff,
Wis provin itself tae be almost, quite an impossible task,

Like Jesus in the wilderness Jim wis vergin oan despair,
He stared at the scrapins o Bitumen, lyin oan the flair,

If only their wis some quick fix, tae clean aff aa this tallow,
Jim wis headin frae the path, that taks the straicht an narrow,

And like his biblical counterpart, his Nemesis noo did alicht,
Toots McCormick, Lucifer incarnate, wi the wiles o an evil sprite,

Some tradesmen will pass ontae boys the knowledge they hae gleaned,
Show ye shortcuts (wi safety in mind), an treat ye like a friend,

But Toots, wi the foul warped mind o a toad,
Wis set tae tak Jim doon the left haun road!

The guid practice learnt in the Trainin Centre, through Jim's mind
    wis racin,
Haudin Tablets o stane (the Safety Code), stood saintly Samuel Mason!

Jim's conscience begged an pleaded, but twas aa tae nae avail,
And here ah pause tae illustrate, oor cautionary tale,

The hills aroond abound wi corpses, hingin oan their fences,
O Moles an Craws wha failed tae heed the fatal consequences,

The Salmon, wi nary a backward look,
Sees the fat juicy worm, never the hook,

The very Deil has Jim by the lug, an at his sleeve he noo dis tug,
Jim gies wan last despairin shrug, then follows Toots oot wi an
    auld pint jug,

'Noo Jim,' says Toots 'there's jist wan thing tae get ye oot this mess,
An seein as yer no lang through, the secret ah'll confess.'

They daundert past the Diesel shed, then by the big Dirt-Hopper,
Then crossin the Woodyaird Toots revealed a secret quite improper,

At the back o the yaird wis a wee brick hut, fenced aff an marked
    'Forbidden'!
Wi a furtive glance Toots produced a key, which he hud carefully
    hidden,

The Woodyaird boys were at their piece, Wee Toots wid never be
    seen,
He emerged fae the hut, the pint jug brimmin, wi illicit
    COALZALENE!

Noo Coalzalene, perhaps ye know, is the fuel that they pit in the lamps,
A precious resource which saved puir souls fae the perils o firedamp,

A highly flammable liquid? an understatement second tae none,
If ye'd pit it in Geoff Dukes Norton he'dve lapped the TT at the ton!

But Jim, his innocent trusting face, oblivious tae sic dangers,
Cairriet the precious liquid back, hidden weel fae pryin strangers,

Back at the binch he stared in awe, as the Coalzalene did the trick,
The Bitumen fairly melted awa, whaur before it'd been fast an thick,

In nae time at aa Jim wis pushin oan, the first twa ends were done,
He sat doon tae his piece, lichten a fag, an thocht 'Ma fortunes turned',

But Bowie appeared, lookin gey thrawn, wi news that hud Jim reelin,
'Wee Toots jist said the Coalzalene shed has been the target o stealin!'

The awfu truth dawned, he'd been duped, how could he hiv been
    sic a fool!
He pictured 'Saint Samuel's gloomy face, at this blatant abuse o the
    rules,

Punishment micht be some far off run,
Whaur the roof wis knee high, an it ran lik a burn,

An that evil wee snake tae Big Davie wid squirm,
Tae mak first claim oan Jim's 'Hill-turn!'

He'd hae tae dispose o the evidence quick,
'Think fast!' or ye'll end up in the Nick!

'But how!?' he desperately socht a plan,
'Ah'll pour the lot doon the lavvy pan!'

'But a quiet toilet?' Jim softly raged,
The yins in the workshop were always engaged,

When he hud the runs it hudnae been fun,
Tae wait tae Big Alex hud feenished the *Sun*,

Management toilets?, not a chance, the scene o misdemeanours,
An he micht disturb an Oversman, shaggin wan o the cleaners!

The Car-Hall hud twae toilets, but a quote fae Big Bob Binnie,
Stated 'Yins lik a dirty protest, in 'A' Hall at Barlinnie!'

The other, paradoxically, could accomodate a Queen,
Saft paper, fitted carpets an a can o 'Mister Sheen!'

This wis the domain o the Banksmen, an guarded like Fort Knox,
Only owr McLatchies body, could ye prise the key fae its box,

Then, with a flash of inspiration,
Jim saw the means tae his salvation,

The Woodyaird toilet wis seldom frequented,
Jim crept an crawled there, hauf demented,

The jug, an Albatross roond his neck, the emblem o his shame,
Wis noo an anathema tae his mind, the source o aa his pain,

But Jim made it through, an skulkin in, he gratefully pued the snib,
'Noo wance ah've poured this doon the pan, Wee Toots'll no be sae
    glib!'

But Jim whase stomach hud churned an gnawed wi this hellish
    agitation,
Wis suddenly grupt by a knot in his bowels, that wid thole nae
    hesitation,

He hauled his boiler suit tae his knees, an plonked his arse oan the pan,
And the peace that passeth all understanding, came owr this
    innocent man,

Jist when he thocht he wis in the clear, the winning post in sicht,
Fate, wi aa his crafty wiles, poured mair misery oan his plicht,

Like Michty Achilles, thon Grecian lad, wha got a richt raw deal,
Jist when he'd smote them hip an thigh, he got it in the heel,

Or Great Goliath wha thocht he'd only, tae skelp some daft wee nyaff,
Got the fricht o his life when a set o slings, near cawed his heid richt aff,

Jim, lost in a reverie of post-excretal contemplation,
His thoughts soaring loftily abune this earthly station,

'Nae mair will ah be duped again, ah'll stick tae the Safety Code,
But afore ah turn a new leaf owr, ah'll hae a fag fir the road!'

Oh Jim, ye've came sae far tae succumb tae this last temptation,
The Coalzalene ablow yer arse will blaw ye tae damnation,

Alas! fir puir Jim, noo he's ran oot o luck,
As the match struck the box he wis blewn tae fuck!!

The Wood yaird boys came runnin oot in wild consternation,
Smoke an flames belched fae the bog, beyond imagination,

Driftin lazily abune the yaird, a plume o black, black smoke,
And wi it the lost innocence of aa a young mans hopes,

But wait, from the grim debris cam a groan that made them falter,
Fae the wreckage a body emerged, wi a toilet seat fir a halter!

Mair deid than alive Jim wis saved, they placed him oan a pallet,
Tae the Medical Centre, gently, puir Jim the cortege cairriet,

Jim hovered twixt life an death, but luckily he recovered,
The dastardly Coalzalene thief, hus never been discovered,

Some inquiries were held, intae the 'Great Woodyaird Explosion',
Such wis the carnage nae clue wis found o Jim Marr's deadly potion,

Wullie Pipers Safety Committee met, tae mak a 'Plan o Action!'
After five meetings (wi lunches o course!), they got satisfaction,

An Inspectors Deputation came, an aa the facts were taen,
The heid yin measured the bog six times (then measured it again!),

An it's strange how things work oot, at least it seems tae me that way,
After makin a thoosand cable-ends, Toots cracked (an wis taen away!),

Jim Marr, ye widnae credit it, hus laughed aa the way tae the bank,
Noo Chief Test pilot (at Barrheid) –
                    EMPLOYED BY ARMITAGE SHANKS!

PART FOUR

'Fair Fa' My Collier Laddie!'

Labour

The bricht rays o the Winter Solstice daws,
Streakin oot owre the Mauchline Basin Plain,
Lichtin oan a slumberin colossus,
The lanely relic o a bygone age.
The horrals o the Barony proudly staun,
Implacable; a great, grey ghaist o steel.
The 'A' Frame, lik some occult wicker-man,
Grim emissary o some auncient god,
Wha, like a god, demandit sweit an tears,
An the bluid o thaim wha wir sacrificed
Oan the altar o Mammon an progress.

They're mindit oan a memorial stane,
The men wha dee'd here, an the men wha leeved.
Twa thoosan pair o eident carefu hauns,
The miners an jiners an engineers,
Wha nevvir aince thocht, as they lauched an joked,
That Fate micht hae a sense o humour tae.
The knowledge they hud sae painfully won,
Wid disappear in that terrible year,
Swept awa bi the haun o history.

Nou the bus drives by wi young Jim an Tam,
Past chain-link fences, roostit 'Keep-Oot' signs,
Oan their wey tae the Technical College.
They ken they're lucky tae hae goat a trade,
It sets thaim apairt frae the ither boys.
The mantle o the village artisan
Is still a badge fir thaim tae wear wi pride;
Council jiners, plumbers or bricklayers,
Electricians, painters an plaisterers.

Aneath thon giant bestridin the yird,
Aneath the lengthnin sheddas o the past,
They'll stoop an gaither up the worn-oot tools,
An forge thaim wi a newer, keener edge,
O Comradeship an Unity an Strength.

Vandals

Thae rioters wha stormed the Millbank Tower,
An smashed up plate gless windaes an the rest,
Aroused the *Telegraph*'s ire, an the *Sun*.
Maraudin students, fechtin wi the polis,
Wha syne wir huckled, cuffed an taen awa.
But frien, ah'm shair, we've seen these fowk afore?
Gin you wid prie their wark, it's there tae see,
They're auld haunds at this gemme o destruction;
Steel-shuttert streets, bulldozed, shattert, gane,
Communities destroyed withooten care,
Skinny pale-faced weans in shoppin centres,
Heroin raddled, destitute, an puir.
Nae joabs, nae howp, nae pride, nae wark, nae dreams.
Luik here, ye'll fin their bitter legacy;
At Cotgrave, Grimethorpe, Ellington, New Cumnock,
Easington, Stainforth, Fallin, Ollerton.
An we aa ken fine weel juist wha they are,
Sae why's there naebody daein ocht aboot it?

Shairpnin Machine Picks

Huncht ower the binch, thick wae metallic stour,
The grinder's wheels sing oot, twal hunner revs,
The hungry pick-boax gants, gleg as a gled;
A galley-slave, chaint fir the neist fowr hours.
Scarf, goggles, helmet, jaiket, buits an gloves,
Glentin wi a sheen o silver ore,
An still ah hear the pitheid gaffer's splore;
'Thon machineman says 'no shairp eneuch'!'
Sae tichten up the angle ten degrees,
Tho fine ah ken they winnae haud their edge,
But ettle gin ah say ocht they'll allege,
'It's that daft boy agane! The yin wha reads!' –
Wha sees reflleckit in the howff's crackt mirror,
The noble dusty face o Christ or Caesar.

The Bagdad Café

'*The Stars are setting and the Caravan*
Starts for the Dawn of Nothing – Oh, make haste!'
—from *The Ruba'iyat* of Omar Khayyam

Bagdad Café, the name daubed oan the door,
O this strange portable caravanserai,
Whaes anely minaret's pickt oot in rid,
Oan this incongruous fremmit prayer rug.
This though's nae Gowden Road tae Samarkand,
The merchants here sell tyres fir dumper trucks,
No silken robes bound fir Byzantium;
The gowd that paves this place is glistenin black.
An here reuch men wull gaither fir tae craic
Anent their rates o pey, or wha's bin sackt,
Ower their coffee, tea or roll oan sausage,
Afore they gang tae mount their big machines
At daw o day, fir aince the stane's bin flung,
As Khayyam sung, that pits the starns tae flicht,
They'll kennle up their beasts an stairt their shift,
Traversin shiftin dunes o shale an earth.
The panoramic windae lets us keek,
Intae the snarlin maw o Bosch's hell,
Wi tiny figures, scurryin to an fro,
Termites pickt oot in yella 'high-vis' jaikets.
Whan aince the hooter's sount tae warn thaim aa,
That shots wull syne be fired, a skinklin flash
Patterns the grund, afore the michty boom,
That brings a towerin cliff face crashin doun;
Then frae their bields they aa come creepin oot,
Resume their mairch oan this weel-trodden road.
Till ae day, whan the coal that's here's bin won,

The hawsers frae some crane wull fasten oan,
An swing her oot, awa ower this great void,
Syne hoist the Bagdad aff tae some new hame;
Whaur the endless darg commences aince agane.

Michty Wheels

(written fir the occasion o the Barony 'A' Frame community launch,
14 June, 2008)

These michty wheels;
wheels o strife,
wheels o life.

Wheels turning anely in oor minds;
that peyed fir Elvis's first LP,
that peyed fir yer first motor-caur,
the holiday in Benidorm or Blackpool.

Like cogs o some gigantic clock
chroniclin oor lives;
cycloid calendar o christenins,
revolvin roond oor mairriages,
that haltit, respectfully,
in heirt-sair seelence,
fir faur ower mony tragic events.

A pendulum o fate,
driven bi cages
fill't wi men.
Lives, held in the balance,
bi slender slivers o raip;
a spider's threid,
that drapt twa thoosan feet,
tae a daurkness unkenned.
Whaur, in some Promethean struggle,
miners wrocht,
tae reive the licht
that sair'd mankind.
But that warld that we kent

is nou aa tint,
e'en its vera language disappearin;
Dowty or dwang,
stable-ends an pans,
main-gate, tail-gate,
tipplers an platefeeders –
an the paraphernalia,
o this titanic industry,
hus aa bin redd awa.

The force that drave its pulse
nae langer viable.

But we, the miners,
we are still stuid here,
aneath these michty wheels,
that still, likesay,
turn in the recess o oor minds –
an hear the echo o a muckle heirt,
still faintly beatin.

The Great Stariski
(a legend o the Barony Colliery)

The Great Stariski maks his entrance bow,
Poised oan the Cross-beam o the vast 'A' Frame;
He aiblins sees imaginary crowds,
Gawpin at his daith-defyin stunts.
Mair's a hunner feet up in the air,
Nae spider's wab o safety-net is strung,
Tae sauf him frae unsocht oblivion.

The Great Stariski luiks tae aa the airts,
Sic magick tricks depend upon their ritual,
An curtly bobs tae each pynt o the compass;
Tae the north, Ben Lomond's silhouette,
Tae the west, Goat Fell oan Arran's isle,
Tae the east, ayont Muirkirk, Cairn Table,
Tae the sooth, Sweet Afton's bonny glen.

The Great Stariski birls an pirouettes,
Then, tae admirin glances frae ablow,
Syne gangs tapselteerie, heelstergowdie,
Stauns oan his haunds, disdainfu o the risks,
An lauchs oot lood in life-affirmin joy
At aa thae wee black specks doun oan the grunnd.

The Great Stariski, balanced oan his girder,
Seems tentless o his parlous circumstance;
Up here he's free, can rax an touch the heivins,
An feel the wuin an rain upon his face.

The Great Stariski leeves athin the moment,
Taks in his queer inversion o the warld,
Syne wi some skeelie dancer's gracefu mien,

Lichtlies doun as saft as thistledown;
Dichts doun his stoorie, creashy overalls,
Sets at a jaunty sklent his auld pit helmet,
Recoups his yirdlie equilibrium,
Descends the ledder – an's mortal aince agane.

Ghaists

Here, oan this blastit hillside, stuid Benwhat,
Whaur haurdy men aince mined the Ironstane,
Till it ran oot – an then they mined fir coal.
Seen frae the heichts it's lyk some Machu-Picchu;
Weird plateaus an mounds define the grunnd,
Strange promontory's grassed ower nou wi green,
As natuir slowly hains back whit's her ain.
Ower-sheddaed by the mammoth Opencasts,
The spoil-heaps o Benwhat are shilpit things;
Worm-casts, neist thae muckle mowdie-hillocks.
That lane brick wa they say wis aince the schuil,
Ah stoop tae lift a waithert block o cley,
'Dalmellington Iron Company', it reads;
The faded legend o some lang loast empire.
There's naethin left o douce, trig miners' raws,
Whaes cobbles rang wi soun o cleek n' girr,
Or scrape o tackets, thud o leather club,
The flap an whirr o racin pigeons wings,
White-peenied weemin clashin ower the dyke;
Whaur yae road taen ye in, an taen ye oot.
Thon aiblins wis 'The Sacred Way' fir some,
Wha laucht an daffed alang it as they left –
When Ne'erday cam, their friens turnt doun a gless.
There's naethin here nou, naethin here but ghaists,
Heich oan the hill the stairk memorial stauns,
A souch o back-end wuin blaws snell an keen,
Throu brucken iron railins, whaur it steirs
The tattert remnants o a poppy wreath.

The Auld Union Banner

Banners sic as this aince flew abune
Battlefields like Bannockburn; Culloden,
Juist as proodly, an wi nae less a purpose.
The uniforms o thaim wha haud it heich,
Oan this braw Simmer's day in Auchinleck,
Are sweatshirt, t-shirt, casual jeans an trainers –
Scotland's fowk, stuill mairchin wi that smeddum
That saw their graundsires bleed fir ither causes;
The Somme, Dunkirk; an e'en Orgreave Cokeworks
(tho medals werenae gien oot fir the latter!).
But the battle an the war is aye the same,
See it here an read it here the day.
These are the people wha focht fir the people,
The graund auld cause that's spelt oot here in rid,
Nae revolution, juist fair shares fir aa.
Ye've mind o thon puir boy wha askt fir mair?
Ah've mind when miners goat the same short shrift,
Frae baton-wieldin bully-boys oan horses,
Wha chairged doun throu the years frae Peterloo.
This banner flew aince at the heid o thoosans,
Led bi Scargill, Clarke, an Mick McGahey,
Sae dinnae think, because the day we're few,
The cause is deid, the struggle bin abandoned,
See it here, an read it here, the day;
Tae Legislate, Educate, aye, an Organise.
Alang Well Road an Barbieston it gangs,
Back Rogerton Crescent, til syne doun past the shoaps,
Whaur auld men stoap, respectfully, tae stare
At an eldritch eemage they'd aamaist firgotten;
Twa miners tyauvin in the mirk o nicht,
Wha'll win throu yet tae tak their share o licht.

PART FIVE

Pit Oot the Lamp

Last Man Standing

In a TV documentary film,
About the UK's social housing crisis,
Robert Brydon stands framed in his doorway,
40 Greenhill Avenue.
A sad defeated pride glistens in his eyes,
For the home he made for his family here;
'Twenty-seven years I've built it up…'
Fond memories of 'guid people',
Whose gardens once so tended, trig and tidy,
Lie overgrown, neglected and abandoned.
His is the last house occupied,
And soon he'll be forced to leave,
The street that rang with laughter and life,
Will see its plug removed, switched off, fall silent.
Decades have passed since the Strike,
Since the last Pit closed,
The kids don't know what a piece of coal is…
It's tough coming home from your work…
Not knowing what to expect…
Wondering if anything has happened…
His interviewer interjects, 'What is home?'
This stoic Tom Joad for our generation,
Gazes to the middle distance, thinking…
'Home means tae me is ah can come hame fae ma work,
Shut the door, come back oot, dae whitevir ah want tae dae,
An come back in an ah ken it's safe enough.
Here, ah cannae dae that'.

The Lost Villages
For Prof Arthur McIvor and Dr Yvonne McFadden

They live only in fading memories now,
These places, Commondyke and Burnfoothill,
Benquhat, Glenbuck, Darnconner, Lethanhill,
Entombed by Opencast, turned by the plough…
And yet, their stories have been teased and told,
The iron range re-lit and brightly glowing,
The steaming washtub, gossipy and knowing,
Treasured memoirs worth their weight in gold!
Schooldays, Sam Purdie vividly regales,
Here's the manager of the Co-op Store,
The football Shanklys, gathered round their door,
Bill's niece, Barbara, relates with pride their tale.
This archive, vital, prescient and profound,
The living proof of what was lost, now found.

The Lost Villages is an oral history project by the Scottish Oral History Centre at the University of Strathclyde, led by researchers Professor Arthur McIvor and Dr Yvonne McFadden. Its aim is to recover the history of East Ayrshire's Lost Villages by collecting the stories of the families who lived in the miners' rows in the villages of Benquhat, Commondyke, Burnfoothill, Glenbuck, Lethanhill and Darnconner. Little, if anything, remains of the villages apart from the living memory of those who lived there. The aim is to reconstruct the social and cultural life of the vibrant coalfield communities that existed in East Ayrshire and the experience of pit closures, depopulation and community disintegration in these so-called 'lost villages'. Telling the story from lived experience; from the memories of those who witnessed working in the coal mines and living in the miners' rows and what it meant when the pits closed. It aims to capture the 'intangible history' of life in the 'row villages' and the impact of deindustrialisation.
https://www.thelostvillages.co.uk/

Coalfields Regeneration Trust

'Give a man a fish and you feed him for a day. Teach him how to fish and you feed him for a lifetime'. Lao Tzu, Chinese philosopher, c. 571 BC

When aince its million warkers aa wir shorn,
Pit villages, destroyed bi callous brutes,
Tuik tent an votit their Tory murderers oot;
An the Coalfields Regeneration Trust wis born.
Its plan, tae bigg communities up agane,
Heal wounds that hud owre lang bin left tae fester,
Instillin hope, life micht fir us be better,
Daicent fowk stept in tae tak the reins,
An syne thair cam a positive force fir chainge;
Training schemes, tae gie us qualifications,
The Walkin Fitba, buildings renovation,
Men's Sheds, or Yoga, Creches fir the weans...
It souns fantoosh, an glossy, but truth be telt,
They jist gie us the tools tae dae't oorsels.

When British coal mining was at its peak in the early 1900s, it was one of the UK's most important industries and employed nearly 1.2 million people. As the industry contracted and large numbers of pits closed, it had a devastating impact on the communities that once relied on them for jobs, housing and social support. By the late 1990s, former coalfield areas had a lack of employment opportunities, experienced high levels of poor health and many people had no or few qualifications. In 1999, The Coalfields Regeneration Trust was established in response to recommendations made by the government's Coalfields Task Force. It was set up as an independent charity with a focus to support the communities and create opportunities for their people.
https://www.coalfields-regen.org.uk/

Dumfries House

Built in the year that Robert Burns was born,
Those in the miners' hovels at Barony Road,
Whose calloused hands had filled each hurlie's load,
Then hauled it to the surface with their brawn,
Had little say in Lord Dumfries's plans,
The Adam Brothers submitted their design,
While you worked twelve hour shifts and lived like swine,
To pay for all his Chippendale divans.
The 5th Earl's wheeze to attract a wife and heir,
Had no success, perhaps he felt 'escheated'?
Nephew, 6th Earl, McDouall, undefeated...
His daughter, Elizabeth, managing to snare,
The Marquess of Bute! And fate's dice kindly roll...
Their fortune built on horn and corn... and coal.

Then, for two hundred years, you gently repose,
Your fading grandeur sleeps through social strife,
Two world wars, decades of Miners' Strikes,
You waken just as Old King Coal's deposed,
And different dirty money's now washed clean,
To build the Chinese Bridge and STEM resources,
There's Art, Wellbeing, Dry Stone Dyking courses,
An Eco-Village proposed, whose cost's obscene.
While scions of those long-forgotten miners,
Can work for Zero Hours in your café,
Or train to be a Butler or Sommelier,
And pour chilled bubbly for Rex and Regina.
Far off the setting Sun the 'A' Frame haunts,
Accusingly at you its shadow points.

The Other Side of Town

'Just a bit of trouble on the other side of town.'
Sir Ian Kinloch MacGregor, chairman, British Coal, in reference to the
1984–85 Miners' Strike.

Knockshinnoch hus its cairn,
Auchengeich its statue.
East Wemyss Michael Colliery fire,
A bleeze that claimed nine miners' lives…
Wis minded mair's fifty year later,
At its wee headframe memorial.
Folk hae mind o their folk in siccan places,
Fir we hae aye luikit eftir oor ain.
An ither bleezes, nae sae langsyne;
At Dundee, Niddrie an Auchinleck,
Kythes the folk wull luik eftir theirsels.
When Britain declared war oan the miners,
Did they think we'd rin the white flag up?
We raised a flag o a different colour…
An focht the guid auld fecht we aye hae focht…
We fecht it nou…
Thae righteous riots alang Sorn Road,
The council flat brunt oot in Old Avenue,
Jist embers fanned bi tyres alowe in '84.
Fir gin yer OCGs an County Lines,
Wid daur tae sell yer pussion tae oor weans,
Div ye'se no think that we'd fail tae chap yer door?
The Polis shuid keep mind whaes side they're oan,
An stowe awa thae shields they uised oan us at Orgreave.
2013: 'Thatcher Dead'. Syne cam the reply,
'SCARGILL ALIVE!'

Deindustrialisation? Mibbes aye... ye'se shut a hauntle Pits,
But, shuttin doun the speerit o the people?
The mining communities wir ne'er defeated,
Jist 'Nursin oor wrath tae keep it waarm...'.
That hardiness bides that boond us aa thegaither,
The social solidarity o oor Schemes,
The Hooch-aye-wha-daur-meddle-wha's-like-us...
Come an hae a go! We're fit fir ye'se yet!

The Deein o the Licht...

Fir a year or twa, eftir ah'd left the Pit,
Gin ah wis in a cupboard, or a place wi puir licht,
An tryin tae see intil some daurk recess or neuk,
Tae aiblins pick some perteecular object oot,
Or read some obscure label or signage,
Ma heid wid tilt unbidden,
Adjust a few degrees, then left or richt...
An instinctual, automatic thing,
It nevir occurred tae me ah wis daein it...
Till the day that it did...
Ah wis tryin tae focus the beam o ma miner's lamp.
It made me feel sad and embarrassed...
Till the day that it didnae...
Then ah'd smile when ah duin it...
It seem't kindae magical!
But ah ne'er let oan tae a sowl.

The Gates at Barony Colliery

The entrance gates to Auschwitz, and other concentration camps, was marked 'Arbeit Macht Frei' (Work sets you free)

The sky was chequer plate Hiduminium,
Clouds, a ladle of cooling white metal,
Stanchions stood erect, while lifeless nettles
Clung, even nature hadn't forgiven them;
These gates, that divided, then conquered men.
Strange, that all has gone, yet these still stand,
A metaphor for our divided land;
While faces half-forgotten from back then,
Leer and taunt; Big Rusty, Harry Parker...
Jibes piercing through the galvanised barbed wire,
The callous Tuesday Boys infernal choir...
January drags me back though, day grows darker...
This paradox here, underscores the lie,
The one we're always told; *'Arbeit Macht Frei'*.

Geothermal
For Professor Zoe Shipton

Mineshafts and roadways would often collapse,
Because water leeched from rocks, ran from streams,
Erupted from unknown aquifers,
Deadly Inrushes from marsh or bog...
A centuries long struggle to keep it at bay,
From Rag and Chain pumps to Multi-Stage Turbines,
But Nature always wins these wars of attrition.
Abandoned mines now assuage an age-old thirst,
Longannet, Cardowan, Killoch, Barony, Polmaise,
Forever submerged great cathedrals of labour,
Face-lines slaked filled with an aqueous dormant darkness,
Hundreds of cubic kilometres, a subterrestrial sea,
Drowned in the sweat of a million men.
Lost as the legendary *Titanic*. Forgotten. Gone.
Till a new age dawned, and a new phrase coined; Green Heat.
Coal smog had clogged our damaged planet's lungs,
No more can we harvest that Paleozoic seam,
No more the anathema of fossil fuels,
Boreholes now tap into latent heat,
The ground itself some giant immersion heater,
And gigawatts of power that was left untapped,
Can now be stored in those pitch black caverns,
That lifetimes ago were carved beneath our feet.
A world those Ayrshire miners never envisioned,
Yet this perpetuates that Promethean flame,
The one that their back-breaking toil strove to fuel,
Their world decarbonised, a future clean and fit for purpose.

Note on 'Geothermal'

ZOE SHIPTON IS Professor of Geological Engineering in the Department of Civil and Environmental Engineering, University of Strathclyde. She researches the influence of faults and fractures on fluid flow in applications such as carbon capture and storage, hydrocarbons and radioactive waste disposal. She is one of the researchers who have won early stage funding to research and develop plans to tap into disused, flooded coal mines for geothermal heat. The British Geological Survey (BGS) are a partner in the consortium for the HotScot project which will share research data, design and drill geothermal boreholes. The consortium is led by the Professor and includes Heriot-Watt, Glasgow and Stirling universities, Townrock Energy, the British Geological Survey, Ramboll UK, Envirocentre, Engie Urban Energy and Synaptec. The project has three core themes: minimising technical, geological, environmental, societal risks; maximising socio-economic benefits; and engaging communities in their energy future. If successful the HotScot consortium will develop at least three new mine-water geothermal heating/cooling/thermal energy storage sites in the Central Belt of Scotland.

Professor Shipton said:

Heat trapped in flooded coal mines represents a vast untapped low-carbon energy resource. The UK's former coal mines are a £3 billion liability, but HotScot can demonstrate how these old mines could become an economic asset. Flooded coal mines contain water with little to no seasonal variation in temperature making them an ideal heat source for district heating networks to support low-carbon, affordable heating, cooling and heat storage for local communities and businesses. The work as part of the HotScot consortium builds on the BGS' research into the development of disused, flooded coal mines for geothermal heating, cooling and storage. The Glasgow Observatory, part of the UK Geoenergy Observatories is the BGS' newest scientific research facility. It is the first of its kind for scientists to take forward research vital to understanding the role that shallow geothermal energy could have in the decarbonisation our energy supply.

A BGS spokesperson said:

We are contributing to the knowledge society needs to achieve net zero. There is a growing community of academic organisations, businesses and public bodies working to realise the potential of mine water geothermal energy and storage. We're proud to be part of that community and helping to tackle the fundamental environmental challenges facing our future.

The above note contains Natural Environment Research Council materials © NERC 2024.

Scots Glossary

A

aa	all
aamaist	almost
aback	after
ablow	below
ablow	beneath
abune	above
ahint	behind
aiblins	perhaps
ain	own
aince	once
alowe	alight
aneath	beneath
anely	only
anent	about
athin	within
auld	old
auncient	ancient
awa	away
aye-an-oan	continue to
ayeweys	always
ayont	beyond

B

back-end	late autumn
bairntid	childhood
bane	bone
baton	thick plank
baur-room	bar-room
beild	shelter
bigged	built
biggit	build
bin	been
birl	spin round
blastit	blasted
blaw	blow
boond	bound
brae	hill
brekkin	breaking
bruck	broke
brucken	broken
brunt	burnt
brushin	road-driving, in mines
bucklet	buckled
buik	book
bunnet	bonnet

C

cauf-kintra	place of birth and early life
caunle	candle
clashin	gossiping
cleek 'n' girr	stick and hoop
cley	clay
courie	snuggle/crouch
couriet	snuggle or shelter
craic	converse
crambo-clink	doggerel, rough, uneven verse
creeshie	greasy
crood	crowd
cundie drain	entrance in a dyke

D

daffed	fun, foolish behaviour
daicent	decent
darg	work
daur	dare
daurk	dark
daurkness	darkness
daurknin	darkening
dee	die

deid	dead
desprait	desperate
dicht	wipe
ding	beat or strike
dinnae	do not
doocot	dove-cot
dug 'n' doo	dog and pigeon
douce	tidy
doun	down
dout	doubt
drapt	dropped
drave	drove
dumfoundit	speechless

E

eemage	image
een	eyes
enow	enough
etcht	etched
ettled	reasoned

F

faur	far
flair	floor
focht	fought
follaed	followed
forleitit	abandoned
fowk	folk
frae	from
fuin	find

G

gane	gone
gang	go
gawpin	gaping
gey	very
ghaist	ghost
gied	gave
gien	given
glaur	mud
gless	glass

gloamin	twilight, dusk
goat	got
gowd	gold
graith	tools, equipment
grew	greyhound
grunnd	ground

H

haimmer	hammer
hained	taken
hain	take
haud	hold
haund	hand
haurdy	hardy
heelstergoudie	head-over-heels
heich	high
heicht	height
heirt-sair	grief-stricken
heirt	heart
heivin	heaven
hemm't	hemmed
hewin	hacking
hinnerend	at the finish-up
hou	how
howff	shelter
howk	dig
howp	hope
hud	had
hunkert	squatting
hunner	hundred
hus	has
howkin	digging

I

intil	into

J

jimp	jump
jynt	joint

K

keek	peek
kent	knew
kirk-yett	church gate
kythe	show, reveal

L

'lad o pairts'	self-taucht
lane	lone
lang-syne	long ago
langer	longer
lauch	laugh
laucht	laughed
laump	lamp
lawin	pay the reckoning
lea	leave
leemit	limit
leeve	live
licht	light
lichtit	lighted
lichtlies	descends
ligg	lie
lockt	locked
lowe	burn, glow
lowsed	loosed, set free
lunky-hole	a hole in a wall
lyk	like

M

mair	more
maist	most
mak	make
mang	among
maw	jaw
michty	mighty
mirk	darkness
mony	many
muckle	big, huge
muin	moon

N

nae	no
naethin	nothing
naitrel	natural
natuir	nature
naukit	naked
Ne'erday	New Year's day
neist	next
nem	name
neuk	nook
nou	now

O

oangaun	event
oor	our
ootby	outside
ower	over

P

peenied	pinafored
peyed	paid
pownie	pony
proodly	proudly
puckle	small amount
puir	poor
puirtith	poverty
pussion	poison
pynt	point

Q

quate	quiet
queer	strange
quey	heifer

R

raip	rope
raison	reason
raw	row
rax	reach
raxin	reaching
redd awa	swept away

redd-up	clean up	stane	stone
reive	plunder/take	staun	stand
reuch	rough	staunin	standing
rid	red	steir	stir
ruif	roof	still-an-oan	even now
		stoorie	dusty
S		stuid	stood
sae	so	suin	soon
saft	soft	sweir	reluctant, unwilling
saicent	second	syne	soon
saicret	secret		
sair	serve	**T**	
sair	sore	tae	to
sair'd	served	taen	took
sairchin	searching	tap	top
sate	seat	tapselteerie	upside-down
schuil	school	tattert	tattered
seddae	shadow	tentless	unaware
seelence	silence	thae	those
seelent	silent	thaim	them
shacklet	shackled	theirsel	themselves
sheddaed	shadowed	tholed	withstood
shilpit	shrunken	thon	that
shoap	shop	thrang	busy
shooder	shoulder	throu	through
shuit	shoot	tint i' the wuin	lost in the wind
sic	such	tint	lost
siccan	such, suchlike	trait	treated
skeelie	skilful	tred	trade
skinklin	twinkling	treidin	treading
sklent	angle	trig	neat
slaw	slow	troot	trout
slawly	slowly	tyauvin	working
smeddum	spirit		
snell	bitterly cold	**U**	
sooth	south	uise	use
souch	sigh	unkenned	unknown
soun	sound	unkent	unknown
sowl	soul		
speerit	spirit	**V**	
stairk	stark	vyce	voice

W

wa	wall
waithert	weathered
wan	one
warld	world
waur	worse
weel	well
weill	benefit
wha	who
whaes	whose
whan	when
whaur	where
wir	were
wis	was
wrocht	created, worked
wrocht	to work
wrocht	worked
wuid	wood
wuin	wind
wull	will

Y

yae	one
yella	yellow
yin	one
yirdit	buried
yirdlie	earthly

Photo Credits

Page 17 – Rab Wilson, aged 22 in 1983, taken in the Car Hall howff (workshop) at Barony Colliery. Credit: Rab Wilson.

Page 21 – Striking miners, taken at Cumnock Juniors Social Club (the local Strike Centre), 1984. Credit: Jim McBlain.

Page 97 – NUM union banner, Barony Branch. Taken at a march in Auchinleck, 2008. Credit: Rab Wilson.

Page 115 – March held in Cumnock in support of the Miners' Strike, Sunday 26 August, 1984. This was a huge rally attended by the main leaders and local political supporters of the Strike; Arthur Scargill, Mick McGahey, George Bolton and George Foulkes MP. Credit: Jim McBlain.

Page 143 – The giant Colliery Winding Gear 'A' Frame at Barony Colliery. The 'Horrals' in mining parlance. The only part of the pit now remaining. 150 feet high, it is preserved as a national monument to Ayrshire's miners and those who lost their lives working at the colliery. Credit: Billy McCrorie via Wikimedia Commons.

Page 157 – Another detail from the March held in Cumnock in support of the Miners' Strike, Sunday 26 August, 1984. Credit: Jim McBlain.

Page 174 – The Miner, a sculpture at the site of the Barony Colliery. Credit: Rosser1954 via Wikimedia Commons.

Luath Press Limited

committed to publishing well written books worth reading

LUATH PRESS takes its name from Robert Burns, whose little collie Luath (*Gael.*, swift or nimble) tripped up Jean Armour at a wedding and gave him the chance to speak to the woman who was to be his wife and the abiding love of his life. Burns called one of the 'Twa Dogs' Luath after Cuchullin's hunting dog in Ossian's *Fingal*. Luath Press was established in 1981 in the heart of Burns country, and is now based a few steps up the road from Burns' first lodgings on Edinburgh's Royal Mile. Luath offers you distinctive writing with a hint of unexpected pleasures.

Most bookshops in the UK, the US, Canada, Australia, New Zealand and parts of Europe, either carry our books in stock or can order them for you. To order direct from us, please send a £sterling cheque, postal order, international money order or your credit card details (number, address of cardholder and expiry date) to us at the address below. Please add post and packing as follows: UK – £1.00 per delivery address; overseas surface mail – £2.50 per delivery address; overseas airmail – £3.50 for the first book to each delivery address, plus £1.00 for each additional book by airmail to the same address. If your order is a gift, we will happily enclose your card or message at no extra charge.

Luath Press Limited

543/2 Castlehill
The Royal Mile
Edinburgh EH1 2ND
Scotland
Telephone: 0131 225 4326 (24 hours)
Email: sales@luath.co.uk
Website: www.luath.co.uk